POWERHOUSE:
PROVEN AI PLAYBOOK TO 10X YOUR BUSINESS AND LEADERSHIP IMPACT

10 Plug-and-Play Artificial Intelligence Driven Business Ideas and Strategies for Aspiring Entrepreneurs and Leaders

Anurag Jain

Chennai • Bangalore

CLEVER FOX PUBLISHING
Chennai, India

Published by CLEVER FOX PUBLISHING 2023
Copyright © Anurag Jain 2023

All Rights Reserved.
ISBN: 978-93-56487-16-1

This book has been published with all reasonable efforts taken to make the material error-free after the consent of the author. No part of this book shall be used, reproduced in any manner whatsoever without written permission from the author, except in the case of brief quotations embodied in critical articles and reviews.

The Author of this book is solely responsible and liable for its content including but not limited to the views, representations, descriptions, statements, information, opinions and references ["Content"]. The Content of this book shall not constitute or be construed or deemed to reflect the opinion or expression of the Publisher or Editor. Neither the Publisher nor Editor endorse or approve the Content of this book or guarantee the reliability, accuracy or completeness of the Content published herein and do not make any representations or warranties of any kind, express or implied, including but not limited to the implied warranties of merchantability, fitness for a particular purpose. The Publisher and Editor shall not be liable whatsoever for any errors, omissions, whether such errors or omissions result from negligence, accident, or any other cause or claims for loss or damages of any kind, including without limitation, indirect or consequential loss or damage arising out of use, inability to use, or about the reliability, accuracy or sufficiency of the information contained in this book.

Table Of Contents

Preface v
About The Author vii
Introduction x

Important Note: Maximizing Your Journey Through This Book 1
Live Case Studies 4
Embracing Change: Why Now Is The Time For Ai 5
Industry-Specific Ai Applications: Real-World Impact 17
Powering The Ai Adoption Flywheel 27
Quick Guide to Prompt Engineering, AI Tools and APIs 39
Be the 10x Leader: Unlock Your Leadership Potential with AI 62
Key Plug-N-Play Strategies For Ai Application In Business – An Introduction 70
Harnessing AI to Revolutionize Market Research & Product Development 78
Branding And Marketing: Supercharged By Ai 97

Table Of Contents

Amplify Your Sales And Business Development With AI 119

AI-Driven Strategy, Planning, And Analytics 135

AI And The Transformation Of Supply Chain Management 152

Revolutionizing Customer Experience And Support With AI 168

The AI-Driven Business Process Automation 183

HR, Learning, Development, And Recruitment In The Age Of AI 202

Going Digital: AI And Your Web, App, Social Media Strategy 217

Beyond The Obvious: AI In Finance, Legal, Project Management, And More 238

Taking The Leap - Embracing AI In Your Business Journey... 252

Mastermind Course - Empowering Your Entrepreneurial Journey with AI 258

BONUS - 10 Ready to Use AI-Driven Business Launch Templates 261

Preface

*A*s we sail into the artificial intelligence (AI) era, a profound transformation is at our doorstep, ushering in a paradigm shift not seen since the dawn of the internet. AI is at the heart of this technological disruption—an extraordinary and pivotal tool reshaping our daily lives and the fabric of our businesses. As the murmurs about AI's potential and ensuing disruptions grow louder, one key question rings out: How can we, today's leaders, move AI from the realm of buzzwords to tangible, actionable tools that amplify our impact and potential by 10x?

In *POWERHOUSE: Proven AI Playbook to 10x Your Business and Leadership Impact*, we explore and demystify AI's realm together. This book is not a dense manual filled with technical jargon but a beacon guiding leaders, entrepreneurs, and anyone intrigued by AI's potential toward harnessing its transformative power. It's a roadmap revealing how AI can propel businesses and individuals towards previously unimagined heights—much like literacy revolutionized society centuries ago.

Today, AI is primarily wielded by tech titans, their deep pockets, and specialized expertise enabling the creation of complex AI systems. Nevertheless, countless small enterprises, from local pizzerias to online T-shirt startups, sit on untapped data goldmines that AI could leverage if only the knowledge and resources were within their grasp. This book addresses this "long-tail" problem of AI, bridging the gap between potential and reality and putting the power of AI within reach of all.

We dive into real-world applications and plug-and-play strategies that you can seamlessly weave into your leadership journey, transforming the theoretical into the practical. From market research and product development to branding, sales, customer experience, and beyond—we examine how AI can influence every facet of your business and personal development.

Furthermore, this book extends an invitation to envision a future where AI is not the bogeyman but an ally—a future where AI enhances rather than replaces human leadership. I implore you to join me in this thought experiment to redefine leadership in the age of AI.

My voyage into AI's fascinating world has been fueled by curiosity, wonder, and a steadfast belief in technology's potential to elevate humanity. This book extends that journey and encapsulates my learnings and experiences. I invite you to embark on this voyage with me to embrace this new era of AI-powered leadership. We will uncover ways to amplify our leadership potential and business impact by 10x.

The dawn of a new leadership era is upon us, inseparably entwined with AI. So, I ask you—are you ready to leap into the future?

Welcome aboard!

Anurag Jain

About The Author

*I*ntroducing Anurag Jain, a seasoned business leader with a strong background in both the consumer and technology industries. With his impressive academic credentials, he has successfully led global operations at top-notch international brands like Johnson & Johnson, Godrej Consumer, Abbott Healthcare, Amazon, and Expedia Group. He has worked in large organizations and startup units, building and advising diverse businesses in industries ranging from fashion to healthcare and from traditional retail to e-commerce. Anurag has helped hundreds of brands and businesses achieve million-dollar milestones.

Anurag's professional journey is a testament to his prowess in transforming nascent business units into thriving, profitable ventures. His proven track record in steering large-scale portfolios, pioneering innovative marketing strategies, and building million-dollar brands from scratch is truly remarkable. His passion for innovation and customer-centric approach have consistently resulted in exponential business growth and scaling of multiple brands over the past two decades.

However, the essence of Anurag's identity is not confined to the boardrooms. His heart beats for technology in business, particularly the transformative potential of Artificial Intelligence (AI). He sees a future where business and AI are inextricably linked, co-evolving and shaping each other's trajectories.

This book, a brainchild of Anurag's unwavering belief in the power of AI for supercharging business growth, is a testament to his vision of a future where technology and business seamlessly intertwine. Through this book, Anurag invites readers to join him on a thrilling journey towards an AI-empowered future for businesses and leaders, promising a world of endless possibilities.

Behind this dynamic leader is a doting father and a loving husband. The unyielding support of his wife has been a cornerstone in his successful journey, and his two children are his greatest joy. A passionate traveler, Anurag believes in enriching his life experiences by exploring the world, one country at a time. A lover of books, a travel enthusiast, and an avid golfer, he cherishes these moments of solitude that give him a sense of calm and help him recharge.

Anurag's story isn't just about a successful career or a passion for technology; it's about balancing professional triumphs with personal happiness. It's about dreaming big, working hard, and never forgetting what truly matters – family, passion, and the pursuit of knowledge. This unique blend of professional prowess, personal sincerity, and emotional honesty makes Anurag a truly relatable author, adding an extra layer of authenticity to his words.

Anurag has also included 10 live case studies in this book, showcasing the implementation of AI tools in various business functions. This provides readers with a hands-on perspective and demonstrates the power of AI. Following the book's guidance is guaranteed to result in a 10x impact across each function. Whether you are an experienced leader, a founder, or an aspiring entrepreneur, this book is an ideal launchpad for exploring the world of AI and business.

Introduction

"Innovation distinguishes between a leader and a follower."
– Steve Jobs

*I*magine you could be in ten places at once. Would you seize the chance to turbocharge your business growth and leadership impact? This question kept me up many nights during my tenure as the leader of a growing business. Juggling multiple roles, from strategizing in high-stakes boardroom meetings to being out in the field connecting with retail partners, I was constantly racing against the clock. Amid the hustle and bustle, I often wondered, "What if I could multiply my efficiency, presence, and impact?"

As days turned into months and months into years, my curiosity about enhancing productivity led me down an unexpected path—artificial intelligence (AI). My unique experiences with traditional and tech-first organizations gave me a front-row seat to the AI revolution sweeping across industries. I witnessed firsthand how AI was an abstract, futuristic concept also a game-changing tool reshaping business and leadership dynamics.

In this ever-evolving business landscape, the power of AI has never been more crucial. The shift from the industrial to the AI era has dramatically changed how we work, operate, and grow. Industries are transforming, businesses are adapting, and those who fail to catch up are fading. AI is the linchpin of a thriving, future-ready business amid all these shifts.

This book is the result of my exploration into the world of AI–a world that enabled me to finally experience the impact of AI on business. It allowed me to streamline my efforts, amplify my impact, and carve out time for what mattered most—innovation and creation. I discovered the strategies, insights, and tools that transformed my leadership and business growth approach. Now, I want to share these learnings with you.

This book is organized around ten strategies that incorporate AI technology and relate to different aspects of business and leadership, such as customer engagement, automation, sales and marketing, and branding. The chapters draw from my extensive experience leading cross-functional teams in various industries and consulting with multiple businesses to achieve success in the digital realm. Whether you are a leader, solopreneur, or aspiring entrepreneur, this book will provide valuable insights to help you succeed.

This book is not a theoretical tome but a practical, hands-on playbook for extracting value, solving challenges, and scaling your impact. It's a journey that will make you think, reflect, and ask, "How can I leverage AI to be my best self?"

So, dear reader, it's time to get ready to blast off on this rocketship I like to call the 'powerhouse.' The time to harness the power of AI and unlock your true potential is now. Let the adventure begin!

IMPORTANT NOTE: MAXIMIZING YOUR JOURNEY THROUGH THIS BOOK

*W*elcome to a comprehensive and practical exploration of the fascinating world of AI and its transformative potential for your business. While this book aims to impart valuable insights and knowledge, it is fundamentally designed to be an active guide for your journey.

This isn't merely a book; it's a toolkit and a conversation. It's not just about learning; it's about application. So, as you navigate through each chapter, remember that your journey will be enhanced when combined with the toolkit I have meticulously put together. This toolkit, referenced throughout the book, is where the theory meets practice. It provides a hands-on approach to applying AI in your business, enriched with practical examples and relevant tools.

The book is split into two main parts: the first focuses on comprehending AI and its various applications, while the second delves into using AI in ten key aspects of business and leadership.

As a bonus, the book also offers ten pre-made AI templates that can be utilized to jumpstart your own business venture.

As you read, keep an eye out for the following icons for additional resources:

💡 Live Case Study – Check out our Online AI Toolkit

This icon signifies that a practical example related to the current topic is available. These real-world live cases will give you a deeper understanding of how concepts play out in actual scenarios.

🛠 AI Tool Referenced

When you see this icon, we're discussing a particular AI tool. I recommend you check out the tool online to gain a deeper understanding of its application for your business and personal growth.

Online AI Toolkit → https://businessaitoolkit.com/powerhouse

Important Note: Maximizing Your Journey Through This Book

You can also access the online toolkit by scanning the QR code above.

Remember, the power of this book lies not in passive absorption but in active engagement. As we embark on this journey together, I encourage you to pause, reflect, and explore the toolkit.

Try out the tools, examine the examples, look up new words, and, most importantly, consider how each insight can be applied to your business.

Let us begin this exciting journey of harnessing AI to supercharge your business and leadership impact!

LIVE CASE STUDIES

AI Integration Across Business Functions

1. AI-Powered Market Research and Product Development 90
2. AI Integration Across Branding and Marketing 111
3. AI-Powered Business Development and Sales 129
4. Harnessing AI for Business Planning, Analytics, and Strategy 145
5. AI-Powered Supply Chain Management 164
6. Leveraging AI In Customer Support and Experience 178
7. AI in Business Process Automation 195
8. Streamlining HR Operations with AI at Sparklabs 212
9. AI-Powered Digital Channel Launch and Scale Up 230
10. Revolutionizing Project Management with AI at Autom8AI 247

EMBRACING CHANGE: WHY NOW IS THE TIME FOR AI

> *"The future depends on what we do in the present."*
> *– Mahatma Gandhi*

*I*magine standing on the edge of an unknown terrain, a vast new world spread before you, promising boundless opportunities. That's where we stand today on the precipice of the AI revolution. Moreover, as with any journey into the unknown, there might be a sense of fear or uncertainty.

But as Mark Twain rightly said, "Twenty years from now, you will be more disappointed by the things you didn't do than by the ones you did do." The future waits for no one. The question is, are you ready to embrace it?

We are at an inflection point in history, witnessing a profound shift towards embracing the power of Artificial Intelligence (AI). Just like the transformation that occurred when people shifted from waiting in long queues to booking trains online, AI has the potential to revolutionize industries and elevate our lives to new heights. At first, the transition to online train bookings might have seemed overwhelming and chaotic, but once experienced, no one yearned to return to the inefficiencies of the past. Similarly, AI was initially a new and complex landscape, but now it is intertwined with our daily routines, making our lives more convenient and efficient.

The convergence of three essential factors has catapulted AI to the forefront of innovation. First, we live in the era of Big Data, generating a staggering amount of information every minute, fueling AI's ability to learn, understand, and predict. According to an IBM study, we produce 2.5 quintillion bytes of data daily—that's 18 zeros! This colossal amount of data is the lifeline of AI, providing it with the necessary fuel to learn, understand, and predict. Second, technological advancements have given us computational power capable of running complex AI algorithms. And finally, the development of machine learning algorithms has seen significant growth, unlocking AI's true potential.

But AI's impact goes beyond the convenience of personalized recommendations or voice assistants. It has the power to supercharge businesses and elevate leadership impact. The AI revolution is not a distant fantasy—it's happening now, reshaping every industry and creating opportunities and strategies for those who embrace it.

It's truly impressive to witness how quickly certain apps can amass 100 million users in a hyper-competitive world! According to Visualcapitalist.com, CHATGPT achieved this remarkable feat in just two months, which caused quite a stir in the tech industry.

It's worth noting that AI-powered apps are now setting records like this with enhanced capabilities. This underscores the importance of large and small businesses embracing AI tools and staying up to date with consumer adoption trends.

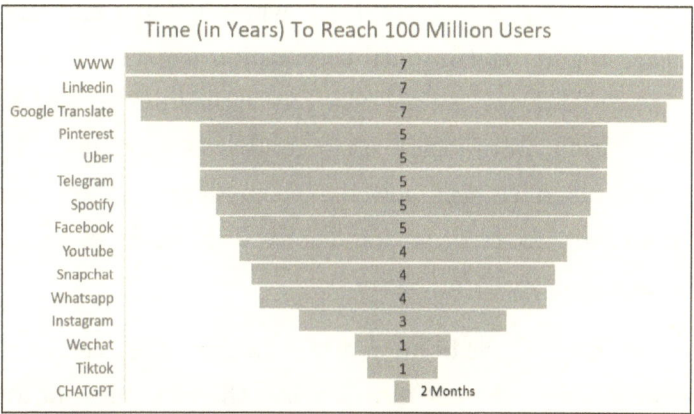

Figure 1 – Approximate time taken for popular apps to reach 100 Million users
(Source – VisualCapitalist.com)

So, fasten your seatbelts and embrace the winds of change, for the AI revolution is here, and it's time to embark on a transformative journey together. Let us equip ourselves with the knowledge and tools to ride the wave of AI-powered progress and emerge as pioneers in this new age of innovation. The future awaits, and the possibilities with AI are boundless—are you ready to seize them? Let's dive in and discover the true POWERHOUSE of AI-driven success!

The AI Revolution: Bridging the Gap Between the Industrial Era and the AI Era

Our world has seen dramatic transformations since the dawn of civilization. We moved from the age of stone to bronze, iron, and steel and journeyed from simple wheel-and-axle mechanisms to steam engines and internal combustion engines. We crossed the threshold from animal-powered agriculture to industrial mechanization, from local bazaars to global e-commerce. Every step we've taken has been powered by one thing—an unwavering thirst for progress. Now, we stand at the brink of the most radical transformation yet—the AI era.

Think of the narrative of humanity as an epic novel, and each era represents a new chapter in this story. The first three industrial revolutions were pivotal chapters, each heralding transformative technologies.

The first revolution was driven by steam power, enabling the mechanization of production. It swapped our reliance on animal and human labor with machinery, setting the foundations for future industries.

The second revolution saw the advent of electricity, making mass production a reality. During this era, Henry Ford and other distinguished people perfected assembly line production, transforming manufacturing as we know it.

The third revolution introduced us to the digital age, characterized by the use of electronics and information technology to automate production. Suddenly, the world was connected, and data flowed like rivers into oceans.

But the story continues. We now find ourselves amid the fourth industrial revolution—an era of extreme automation and ubiquitous connectivity. This revolution, distinct from its predecessors, will blur the lines between the physical and digital ecosystem. And the protagonist of this shift? Artificial Intelligence.

Imagine AI as a bridge that connects us from the remnants of the industrial era to the dawn of an entirely new epoch. A bridge that helps us traverse the gap and transforms us in the process. That's the magnitude of AI's influence.

Amid this transformation, thousands of startups globally now have AI as a core business model.

Tech behemoths are racing towards AI supremacy, betting their futures on this new frontier, and many AI applications have become a part of our daily lives.

But, like a double-edged sword, the effects of AI can be twofold. It can lift those who adapt and sink those who resist.

As Kevin Kelly, co-founder of WIred magazine, said, "The business plans of the next 10,000 startups are easy to forecast: take X and add AI." For the leaders of tomorrow, understanding and harnessing AI isn't just a competitive advantage—it's a matter of survival.

Our world is being reshaped by AI's hand, and the only question that remains is this: Will we cross the bridge into the AI era or watch from the sidelines as the future unfolds?

Remember, the bridge to the AI era isn't a one-way journey. It's a path we can travel back and forth, learning and adapting as we go. AI is not a force to be feared but rather a tool to be harnessed.

The future of AI is a tale yet unwritten, and we hold the pen.

Welcome to the dawn of the AI era. It's time to write the next chapter in our collective narrative.

As we continue our journey, it's essential to understand the technology driving this revolution. In our next chapter, we'll decode some key AI terms critical for a business leader to understand.

AI Deconstructed: Understanding the AI Lingo

In the world we are delving into, where businesses flourish in the age of AI, it's crucial to grasp the tools fueling this transformation. Technologies such as AI, Machine Learning (ML), Generative AI, and Large Language Models (LLM) are more than just buzzwords; they are the pillars supporting the seismic shift in our society. Let us demystify their meaning and significance.

AI: The Seed of the Revolutions

Artificial Intelligence, or AI, is a broad term that denotes machines or software displaying human-like intelligence. It encompasses creating systems capable of tasks requiring human intelligence – learning, problem-solving, pattern recognition, and decision-making. Whether it's a chatbot addressing your questions or an algorithm suggesting the optimal commute route, AI is the driving force.

In 2023, AI's applications are vast. In E-commerce, it powers personalized shopping experiences, fraud prevention, and AI assistants. In the automobile sector, AI enhances in-vehicle experiences and propels self-driving vehicles.

Machine Learning: The Offspring of AI

Machine Learning, a pivotal subset of AI, involves using algorithms to parse data, learn from it, and subsequently make predictions or decisions based on that data. If AI is the seed, ML is the sapling, sprouting from AI's foundational concept.

ML boosts efficiency, curtails costs, and refines customer service across industries. It paves the way for innovative products, task automation, and cognitive functions.

Supervised, Unsupervised, and Reinforcement Learning: The Trinity of ML

Within ML, there are three primary learning methods:

Supervised Learning, where algorithms learn from labeled data.

Unsupervised Learning, where algorithms discern patterns and relationships in unlabeled data.

Reinforcement Learning is a mechanism where an agent interacts with its environment, producing actions and receiving rewards or penalties. The agent learns by maximizing the rewards it garners for its actions.

Generative AI: The Artist of the AI World

Generative AI can craft content that's both novel and convincingly human-like. From generating art and music to drafting emails or crafting prose, it's the AI realm's creative maestro.

In business, generative AI aids in content creation. For instance, in marketing, it supports targeted ads and content creation, while chatbots enhance customer service.

Large Language Models (LLMs): The Linguists in the AI Universe

Large Language Models, like GPT-3, are a subset of generative AI. Trained on a vast array of internet text, they generate human-like text based on given contexts. LLMs are the AI universe's linguists, crafting text with astonishing naturalness.

LLMs enhance customer interactions, with AI-powered chatbots refining user engagements across various sectors.

Artificial General Intelligence (AGI): The Ultimate Goal

Artificial General Intelligence, or AGI, represents the zenith of AI aspirations. Often termed "strong AI," AGI would be as adept as a human in any intellectual task. Unlike today's "narrow AI" tailored for specific tasks, AGI would comprehend, learn, and apply its knowledge across diverse tasks, potentially outpacing human intelligence.

While AGI remains theoretical, current AI advancements edge us closer to its realization. For instance, AI's role in healthcare spans complex tasks like disease detection and drug discovery.

Deep Learning: The Deep Roots of AI

Deep Learning, a subset of machine learning, employs neural networks with many layers to analyze data. It's the powerhouse behind many advanced AI applications today, from voice assistants to image recognition systems.

For instance, tools like AlphaSense offer an AI-powered search engine, enabling investment firms to dissect financial data efficiently in the financial sector.

Natural Language Processing (NLP): The Voice of AI

Natural Language Processing, or NLP, is AI's voice. It empowers computers to understand, interpret, and manipulate human language, fostering communication in intuitive ways. Central to LLMs and many AI applications, NLP is the bridge between machines and human language.

Computer Vision: The Eyes of AI

Computer Vision, another AI pillar, serves as the eyes, allowing AI to interpret and understand the visual world. It's pivotal in enabling AI to interact with its surroundings, from guiding autonomous vehicles to image recognition systems.

For instance, retail establishments like Whole Foods employ computer vision for checkout-free systems.

Ethical Considerations: The Conscience of AI

While not a branch of AI, the ethical ramifications of AI are integral to our exploration. As we navigate AI's transformative impact on businesses and society, we must confront issues like AI bias, its influence on employment, and privacy concerns. AI's conscience reminds us that immense power necessitates immense responsibility.

As we journey further, remember that these aren't mere technical jargon. They're the building blocks of a future where businesses thrive through the harmonious melding of technology and human creativity. Prepare for a riveting exploration of AI in the business realm!

Embracing the AI Era - Opportunities and Strategies for Business Leaders

Welcome to the cusp of a revolution. A revolution not of guns and roses but of algorithms and data. A process that is poised to redefine the fabric of our businesses, economies, and lives. Welcome to the AI era. The artificial intelligence market is already a 454 billion dollar market in 2022 and is on a supercharged growth trajectory, with growth predicted at a compound annual growth rate of 19% from 2022 to 2032 (Source – Precedence Research).

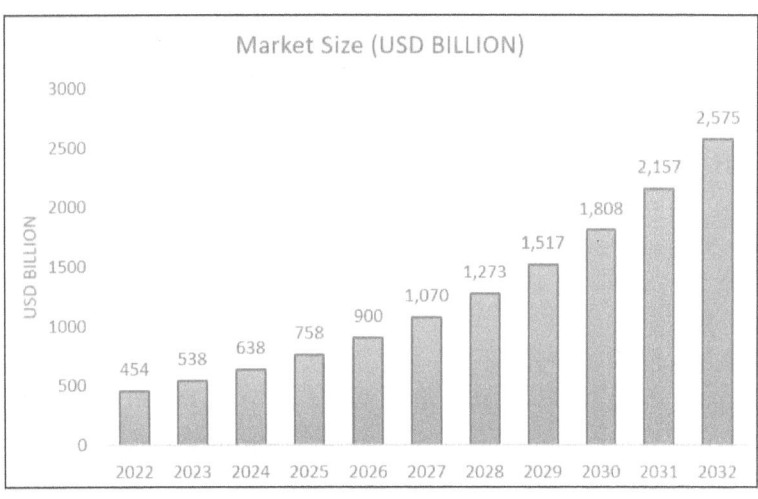

Figure 2 - AI Market Size in Billion USD
(Source - Precedence Research)

As we stand on the brink of this new world, we are not just spectators but active participants. We are the architects of this new reality, the pioneers of this new frontier. As leaders, we can shape this revolution, harness its potential, and steer our businesses into a future of unprecedented growth and prosperity.

But the question remains: How do we navigate this brave new world? How do we tap into the vast opportunities presented by AI and translate them into tangible success? Let us chart our course.

The AI Mindset: Before anything else, we must cultivate the 'AI Mindset.' This isn't about treating AI as just another tool in our tech arsenal. It's about understanding AI as a monumental shift, a game-changer that will infiltrate every corner of our businesses. Embracing change, fostering relentless innovation, and nurturing a thirst for the unknown are essential.

Investing in AI Talent: The journey through the AI landscape requires skilled navigators. Enter the data scientists, AI engineers, and machine learning experts. These trailblazers will be our compass, ensuring we remain at the forefront of this revolution.

Data as Fuel: In this era, data is the lifeblood of our ventures. It's the catalyst that propels us forward, offering invaluable insights into customer behaviors, market dynamics, and operational efficiencies. In the AI realm, data isn't just a tool; it's a powerhouse.

AI Integration: AI's potential is boundless, touching every facet of our organizations. From marketing to HR, AI's transformative power is undeniable. The future belongs to AI-centric businesses, poised to flourish in this new age.

Ethical AI: With great power comes great responsibility. As we harness AI, we must do so with integrity. This means building AI systems that are transparent, fair, and respectful of privacy. Trust is the cornerstone of AI's future.

Adapting to Change: The AI era is dynamic and ever-evolving. Agility, foresight, and innovation are our best allies, helping us stay ahead and capitalize on new opportunities.

Empowering the Workforce: AI isn't about replacing humans but elevating them. By automating mundane tasks, we free our teams to focus on strategic initiatives, fostering a culture of creativity and innovation.

Collaborative Innovation: The AI journey is one best traveled together. We can stay at the cutting edge of AI advancements by forging partnerships with AI solution providers, industry leaders, and academic institutions.

Continuous Learning: In the AI era, the learning curve is perpetual. We must champion a culture of continuous upskilling, ensuring our teams are always in sync with the latest trends and technologies.

In conclusion, the AI revolution isn't about sidelining human intelligence but amplifying it. It's about harnessing AI to enhance our capabilities, making us sharper, more efficient, and infinitely more innovative. As we stand on the precipice of this new era, the question isn't whether we will join the revolution but how we will lead it. The AI era beckons. Are you ready?

INDUSTRY-SPECIFIC AI APPLICATIONS: REAL-WORLD IMPACT

> *"The biggest risk is not taking any risk... In a world that's changing quickly, the only strategy guaranteed to fail is not taking risks."*
> *– Mark Zuckerberg*

Industry Applications

Welcome to a world where the horizon of possibilities stretches beyond the imaginable, where the traditional norms are being redefined, and where every industry is on the brink of a transformative revolution. This is not a figment of imagination but the tangible reality of the AI era we are entering.

AI is not just a buzzword anymore; it's a game-changer making a profound impact across many industries. In this section, we will embark on a journey to explore how AI is revolutionizing various industries with real-world applications that are transforming the way we work, live, and play.

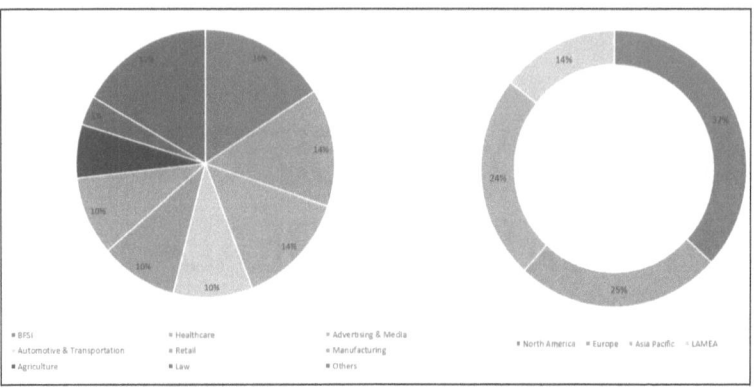

Figure 3 - AI Market Split By Industry and Geography
(Source - Precedence Research)

The healthcare, BFSI (Banking, Financial Services and Insurance) and advertising industries already have been significantly affected and influenced by AI. This impact continues to spread into other industries as well. Even when we look at the geographic statistics, while North America has the largest presence of AI, Asia Pacific is expected to grow the fastest in the next decade on the AI front.

Let us begin with **healthcare** where AI enables data mining, medical imaging, drug discovery, preliminary diagnosis, virtual nursing assistance, and even robotic surgery. AI-powered diagnostic tools can now detect diseases like cancer at an early stage, potentially saving millions of lives. Telemedicine, powered by AI, is democratizing access to healthcare, making it available to those in remote areas.

In the **manufacturing industry**, AI is ushering in a new dawn. With the advent of AI-powered predictive maintenance, machines can anticipate breakdowns before they happen, minimizing downtime and improving productivity. Simultaneously, AI enables a new wave of personalization, allowing manufacturers to create bespoke products at scale. The industry also leverages AI to address supply headwinds, labor shortages, and economic uncertainty.

In **retail**, AI uses predictive analytics to anticipate customer buying behavior, enabling retailers to offer personalized recommendations. For instance, Netflix's recommendation algorithm is a prime example of how AI can enhance customer experience. AI also streamlines supply chain operations, helping retailers maintain optimal stock levels and minimize waste.

The **finance industry** is experiencing an AI revolution, with AI-powered algorithms able to analyze complex data sets, predict market trends, and assist in decision-making. For instance, Q.ai's AI-driven Investment Kits offer automated portfolio management, data analysis, and risk management, ensuring smarter investing and financial rewards.

AI is making a significant impact in **agriculture** as well. Precision farming, powered by AI and IoT, enables more efficient utilization of resources, resulting in increased yields and sustainability. AI can analyze weather patterns, soil conditions, crop maturity, and more, allowing farmers to make data-driven decisions.

In the field of **education**, AI is providing personalized learning experiences. AI-powered platforms can adapt to a student's unique learning style, pace, and preferences, making education more engaging and effective. It also automates administrative tasks and creates innovative content.

AI is pivotal in the **transportation industry**, particularly in developing self-driving cars. AI algorithms are used for safe navigation, traffic management, and predictive maintenance, making transportation safer and more efficient.

In the **real estate sector**, AI tools are used to analyze the housing market for pricing and forecasting, helping real estate agents make informed decisions.

AI is utilized in the **environmental sector** to understand and address environmental issues, such as monitoring global deforestation and optimizing clean energy. Countries and regions are taking steps to decarbonize industries and leverage clean technology manufacturing.

Being in the **travel industry**, I see a profound impact of AI on travel and tourism. From personalized travel recommendations to intelligent booking systems, AI ensures a seamless journey for travelers. AI-powered chatbots assist travelers in real time, addressing queries and offering solutions, while predictive analytics help airlines and hotels optimize pricing based on demand. Virtual reality, backed by AI, offers virtual tours, allowing travelers to experience destinations before booking. Furthermore, AI-driven language translation tools are breaking down language barriers, making international travel more accessible and enjoyable. In essence, AI in the travel industry is not just about streamlining operations but enhancing the entire travel experience, making it more personalized, efficient, and memorable.

These examples are just the tip of the iceberg. Every sector, from logistics to entertainment, feels AI's transformative power. The common thread across all these sectors is the potential for increased efficiency, improved decision-making, and enhanced customer experiences.

The AI Adoption Curve

We will witness an even more significant transformation as we delve deeper into the AI era. The clock is ticking, and the urgency to embrace AI has never been more pressing. Whether you are a healthcare provider, a manufacturer, a retailer, or a farmer, the time to harness the power of AI is now.

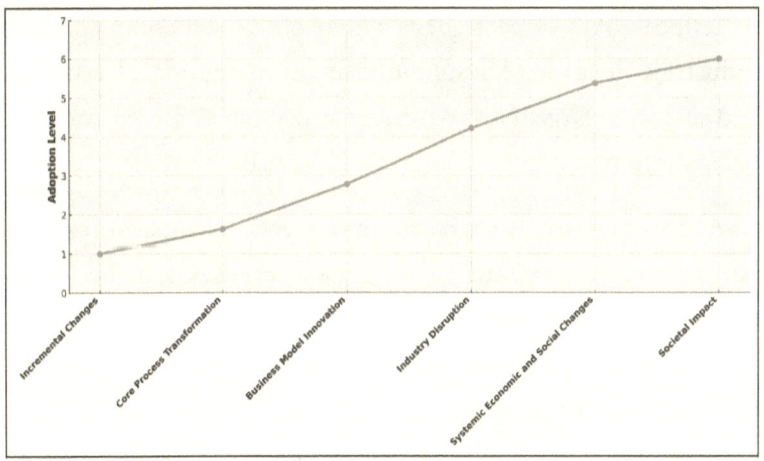

Figure 4 - AI Adoption Curve

The AI adoption curve often begins with incremental changes, where businesses incorporate AI in specific processes or departments. These changes may involve using AI algorithms for data analysis, customer service, or automation of routine tasks.

As businesses gain confidence and experience with AI, they explore its potential to transform core processes. AI is integrated into multiple areas, streamlining operations, improving efficiency, and enhancing decision-making.

Next, at the stage of business model innovation, companies leverage AI to innovate their business models. AI enables the development of new products and services, leading to revenue growth and increased competitiveness.

With AI maturing and demonstrating its transformative power, it can disrupt entire industries. Companies comprehensively embracing AI can outperform their competitors and reshape the market landscape.

At its peak, AI's impact goes beyond individual companies and industries. It leads to systemic changes in the global economy and society at large. New AI-driven ecosystems emerge, fostering collaboration and innovation on a large scale.

As AI becomes deeply ingrained in our lives, its impact on society becomes more pronounced. From advancements in healthcare to environmental sustainability, AI's societal impact reaches far and wide, addressing pressing challenges and creating new opportunities for progress.

AI Application to Businesses of All Sizes

In the grand tapestry of the business world, AI has emerged as a transformative thread, weaving its way through enterprises of all sizes and sectors. From the towering tech titans to the humble local coffee shop, AI is becoming integral to the business fabric, driving innovation, efficiency, and growth.

The AI Landscape: Titans of Tech in the AI Race

In the dynamic realm of artificial intelligence, tech giants like Google, Microsoft, OpenAI, Meta, and IBM are leading the charge. OpenAI, with its GPT-4 model and Microsoft's collaboration, exemplifies the rapid advancements in the field. Google, not to be outdone, has introduced its Bard AI chatbot, showcasing its prowess in conversational AI.

Meanwhile, Meta is pushing boundaries with its Llama 2 model, and companies like Apple and IBM are making significant strides. The year 2023 has also spotlighted other major players, including Nvidia, known for its processing prowess, Baidu, a leader in Chinese internet searches, and Amazon, with its deep commitment to AI through services like AWS.

The competitive landscape of AI in 2023 mirrors the intensity of the Cold War, with Google and Microsoft at the forefront. Microsoft's multi-billion dollar investment in OpenAI and its integration into products like Bing signifies its aggressive AI stance. On the other hand, Google, under Alphabet, has unveiled its Bard AI chatbot and invested heavily in AI research, showcasing its commitment to leading the AI race.

As the AI race accelerates, it's not just about groundbreaking innovation but also the perfection of existing models. With each tech behemoth vying for dominance, the world watches with bated breath, anticipating the next monumental leap in this AI tug-of-war.

Large Businesses

In the intricate game of artificial intelligence, several global giants are positioning their pieces with strategic precision, aiming to checkmate the competition. These titans, reminiscent of the grandmasters in chess, are leveraging AI to redefine the boundaries of technology and commerce.

Alibaba, the Chinese e-commerce behemoth, employs AI to predict customer preferences, auto-generate product descriptions, and even manage traffic in smart cities. Google's parent company, Alphabet, has made significant strides with Waymo, its self-driving technology division, and the introduction of Google Duplex. This AI voice interface can make phone calls autonomously. Amazon, the global e-commerce leader, harnesses AI not just for its voice assistant, Alexa, but also for predictive analytics, anticipating customer needs even before they arise. Apple, the tech innovator, integrates AI into its products, from iPhone's FaceID feature to the smart assistant Siri. Meanwhile, Meta employs AI to structure its vast amount of unstructured data, using tools like DeepText for text understanding and DeepFace for facial recognition.

IBM, a pioneer in the AI realm, has showcased its prowess with feats like the Watson computer winning "Jeopardy" and the recent Project Debater. JD.com, often dubbed the Chinese Amazon, envisions a future of complete automation, with AI-driven drone deliveries already in action. With AI at the core of its vision, Microsoft infuses intelligent capabilities into its myriad products and services. Lastly, Tencent, the Chinese social media giant with its vast user base on WeChat, is expanding its AI reach into diverse sectors, from gaming to self-driving cars.

As these tech giants maneuver their pieces on the AI chessboard, they're not just competing for dominance but are shaping the future of technology, commerce, and society. Their moves today will determine the course of AI's integration into our daily lives, making every strategic play crucial in this grand game.

These tech giants are not just using AI; they are living it, breathing it, and shaping it, creating a ripple effect that's felt across industries and around the globe.

Small Businesses:

As AI continues to democratize, it's beginning to permeate the realm of small businesses, much like the spread of literacy in bygone eras. Picture a local coffee shop or a boutique clothing store. They generate a treasure trove of data daily—from popular coffee beans to peak customer hours or fashion trends to optimal product placement. With AI, this data transforms into a goldmine of insights, helping optimize operations, predict trends, and enhance customer experiences.

The democratization of AI is a revolution in its own right, making AI accessible to even small businesses. It's a shift from the traditional, code-heavy AI development to more accessible methods that prioritize data provision. This shift empowers small businesses to leverage AI, leading to more efficient operations, time savings, and profit growth.

Solopreneurs:

For solopreneurs, AI is like a secret weapon. It automates administrative tasks, provides insights into customer behavior, and helps streamline operations. AI-powered tools like chatbots can handle customer service, while AI-driven analytics can provide valuable insights into market trends and customer preferences.

AI is not just a tool for solopreneurs; it's a partner, a silent collaborator who is always on, always learning, and always ready to provide valuable insights. From social media analysis to email marketing automation, AI is helping solopreneurs optimize their businesses and drive growth.

In conclusion, by embracing the power of AI, businesses can unleash innovation and tackle humanity's most pressing challenges. While the road ahead is undoubtedly challenging, its possibilities are exciting and limitless. Let us embark on this journey together.

POWERING THE AI ADOPTION FLYWHEEL

> *"Technology, like art, is a soaring exercise of the human imagination."*
> *– Daniel Bell*

*I*n the age of digital transformation, the rise of artificial intelligence (AI) and machine learning (ML) has opened up a world of business possibilities. These technologies have the potential to revolutionize industries, offering unprecedented insights and capabilities that can drive informed decision-making, enhance operational efficiency, and provide a competitive edge. However, the journey to AI adoption has its challenges. It requires a robust, sustainable strategy that can guide businesses through the complexities of AI integration and ensure long-term success.

This chapter introduces the AI Adoption Flywheel. This model is designed to help businesses navigate their AI adoption journey effectively and efficiently, focusing on four interconnected pillars: people, process, data, and technology.

The AI Adoption Flywheel signifies a self-reinforcing loop of these critical actions. Just like an actual flywheel that builds up momentum and becomes increasingly efficient as it spins, the components of the AI Adoption Flywheel feed into each other. Your AI adoption efforts become increasingly influential as your organization becomes more proficient in these areas.

To further streamline this process, we introduce the ENABLE framework. This acronym encapsulates the critical aspects of the AI adoption journey and serves as a vital turning mechanism of the AI Adoption Flywheel. It provides a comprehensive, adaptable, and technology-agnostic roadmap for organizations aspiring to become fully AI-powered entities.

As businesses progress in their AI adoption journey, they typically move through three phases of AI maturity: tactical, strategic, and transformational. Understanding these phases and where your organization currently stands can help tailor the ENABLE framework to your needs, making it an efficient roadmap for your AI journey.

However, adopting AI is not just about integrating new technologies but also managing change. Drawing inspiration from Kotter's Change Management Model, I have created an AI Adoption Management Model. This tailored approach addresses the peculiar challenges and opportunities of integrating AI into your business. It provides a step-by-step guide to successfully implementing AI technologies, from creating a sense of urgency for AI adoption to anchoring AI adoption for long-term success.

The following sections will delve into each component, providing a comprehensive guide to powering the AI Adoption Flywheel.

The AI Adoption Flywheel: People, Process, Data, and Technology

The AI Adoption Flywheel is a model that encapsulates AI adoption's cyclical and interconnected nature. It comprises four pillars: people, process, data, and technology. Each pillar is not an isolated entity but is deeply intertwined with the others, creating a self-reinforcing loop that drives the organization's AI adoption forward.

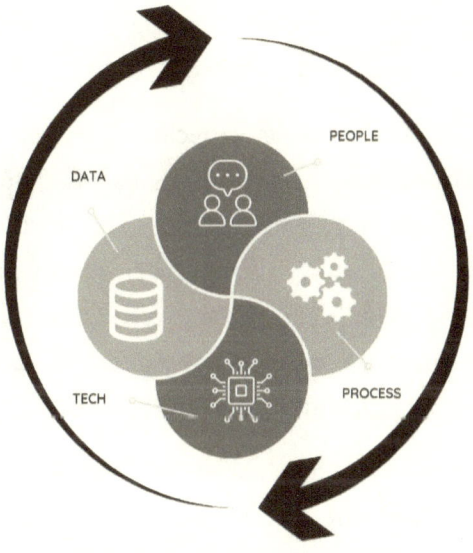

Figure 5 - AI ADOPTION FLYWHEEL

People are the driving force behind AI adoption. They are the ones who identify opportunities for AI deployment, develop and implement AI solutions, and make decisions based on AI-generated insights. Businesses must invest in AI literacy programs, provide ongoing training and support, and foster a culture encouraging curiosity, innovation, and ethical AI use to ensure people can effectively perform their roles.

Processes are the mechanisms through which AI is integrated into the business. They govern how AI projects are initiated, managed, and evaluated. To embed AI in the company›s core processes, organizations must establish clear protocols for AI project management, create cross-functional teams to oversee AI initiatives and develop a framework for scaling AI projects. This might involve redesigning workflows to accommodate AI, implementing new decision-making protocols based on AI insights, and establishing a framework for scaling AI projects.

Data is the lifeblood of AI as AI technologies use data to learn, make predictions, and generate insights. Therefore, a robust data management strategy is crucial. This includes ensuring data quality, establishing strong data governance practices, and complying with data privacy regulations. Furthermore, organizations need to develop procedures for collecting and storing data in an efficient, secure, and scalable way.

Technology is the tool that enables AI adoption. It includes the AI algorithms, hardware, and infrastructure to process data and generate insights. The organization›s specific needs and goals depend on selecting the right AI technologies. This includes considering the scalability of the AI solutions, their compatibility with existing systems, and their ability to deliver the desired outcomes.

The interplay between these four pillars sets the AI Adoption Flywheel in motion. People develop and adapt processes that utilize technology to interpret data. The insights from

this data then inform the people on how to improve their operations and use of technology. Once set in motion, this loop continues to spin, driving the organization's AI adoption forward.

The ENABLE Framework: A Roadmap for AI Adoption

The ENABLE framework is a strategic approach to AI adoption that aligns with the AI Adoption Flywheel, and is inspired from Google playbook. It provides a comprehensive, adaptable, and technology-agnostic roadmap for organizations aspiring to become fully AI-powered entities.

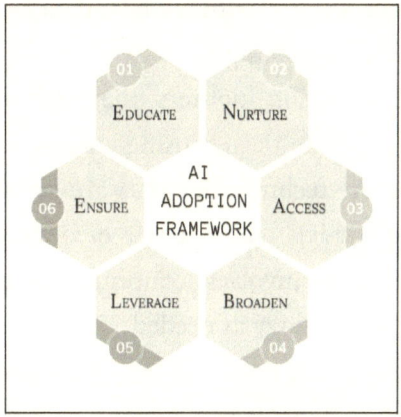

Figure 6 - AI Adoption Framework

The acronym ENABLE stands for:

1. **Educate**: This action strengthens the 'people' pillar. It involves educating and training the workforce to understand and leverage AI. This could involve formal training programs,

workshops, or on-the-job training. The goal is to equip employees with the skills and knowledge needed to use AI effectively in their roles.

2. **Nurture**: This action reinforces the 'process' pillar. To successfully implement AI, it's essential to establish a supportive environment. This includes gaining leadership support, fostering an innovative culture, and providing resources for AI endeavors. Additionally, it's necessary to encourage cross-departmental collaboration on AI projects.

3. **Access**: This action fortifies the 'data' pillar. It refers to the accessibility and quality of data. This involves establishing strong data governance practices, ensuring data quality and integrity, and making data accessible to those who need it. It also involves creating a culture where data is valued and used to inform decision-making.

4. **Broaden**: This action bolsters the 'technology' pillar. It involves scaling AI initiatives using cloud-native technologies and selecting AI technologies that are scalable, compatible with existing systems, and capable of delivering the desired outcomes. It also involves continuously monitoring and updating the technology as needed.

5. **Leverage**: This action boosts all four pillars, with an emphasis on 'technology.' It involves automating data processing and ML pipelines to increase efficiency and effectiveness. This includes automating repetitive tasks, using AI to analyze large volumes of data, and leveraging AI to make predictions and generate insights.

6. **Ensure**: This action also benefits all pillars, primarily 'people' and 'data.' It involves protecting and responsibly using data and AI services. This includes complying with data privacy

regulations, ensuring the ethical use of AI, and establishing trust with stakeholders.

The ENABLE framework encapsulates a holistic approach to AI adoption, ensuring that every facet of an organization is primed for the AI revolution. From nurturing the human element with education to leveraging cutting-edge technology, this roadmap is designed to guide businesses through the intricate journey of AI integration.

As we move forward, we must remember that AI adoption isn't just about technology; it's about aligning people, data, processes, and technology to a unified vision. With the ENABLE framework as a guide, organizations are better equipped to harness AI's transformative power and confidently navigate the future.

Having established a foundation with the ENABLE framework, let us delve deeper into the AI Maturity Phases to understand the progression of AI integration in organizations.

AI Maturity Phases: Tactical, Strategic, and Transformational

The AI Maturity Phases represent the progression of an organization's AI adoption journey. They provide a roadmap for organizations to follow from initial AI adoption to becoming a fully AI-powered entity.

In the *tactical* phase, organizations are just beginning their AI journey. They are exploring AI technologies and using them for simple, short-term use cases. The focus is on getting quick wins and learning from these initial experiences. Organizations may have a short-term strategic plan for AI adoption at this stage.

In the *strategic* phase, organizations have moved beyond initial exploration and are using AI to deliver sustainable value. They have several ML systems in production and use AI as a strategic business enabler. At this stage, organizations have a clear vision for AI adoption and are actively working towards it.

In the *transformational* phase, AI has become pivotal to the organization. It drives innovation, cultivates continuous learning and experimentation, and transforms the organization›s operations. At this stage, organizations are not just using AI; they are continuously improving and expanding their use of AI.

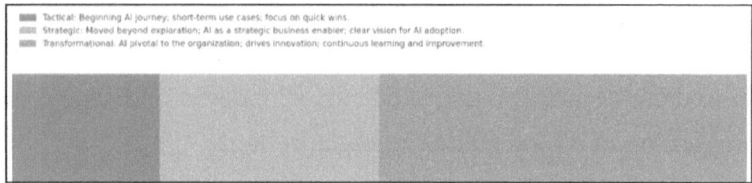

Figure 7 - AI Maturity Phases for a Business

Understanding the AI Maturity Phases becomes paramount as organizations navigate the intricate maze of AI adoption. From the tactical phase's initial steps to the transformational phase's profound integration, this journey is not just about technology adoption but a holistic transformation of organizational processes, mindset, and vision. It's a metamorphosis from being AI-curious to AI-centric.

As we transition to the next section, "The AI Adoption Management Model," we will delve deeper into the strategies and frameworks that can guide organizations seamlessly traverse this path, ensuring that their AI endeavors translate into tangible success.

The AI Adoption Management Model: Navigating the Path to AI Success

The AI Adoption Management Model is a step-by-step guide to successfully implementing AI technologies. It is inspired by Kotter's Change Management Model and is tailored to address AI adoption's unique challenges and opportunities.

Let's delve into these steps with an example of a large, traditional retail company that wants to leverage AI to improve its operations and customer experience. We'll call this company "RetailCo."

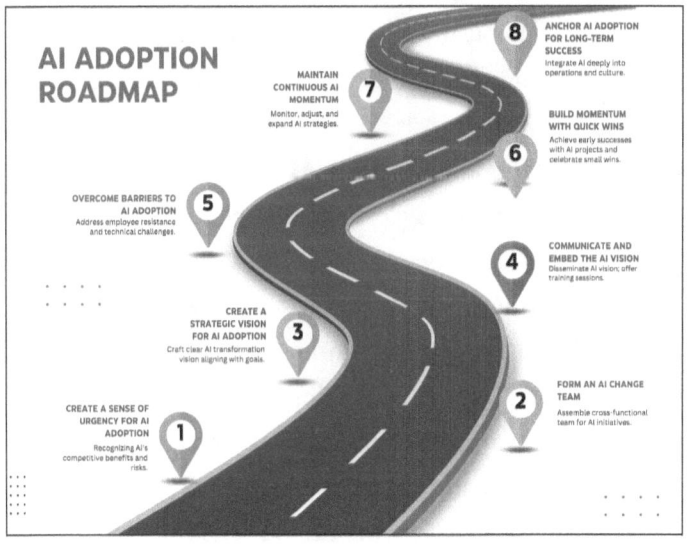

Figure 8 - AI Adoption Roadmap

1. **Create a Sense of Urgency for AI Adoption:** The first step is to create a sense of urgency around AI adoption. This involves communicating the benefits of AI and the risks of not adopting it. For example, RetailCo›s leadership recognizes that the competitive landscape is changing rapidly with e-commerce and other retailers using AI to personalize customer experiences and streamline operations. They communicate this urgency to the entire organization, highlighting the risk of falling behind competitors and AI's opportunities to improve customer service and operational efficiency.
2. **Form an AI Change Team:** The next step is to assemble a team of individuals who will lead the AI adoption effort. This team should include individuals with diverse skills and perspectives. RetailCo forms a cross-functional AI Change Team comprising representatives from IT, data analytics, marketing, sales, and operations. This team is tasked with leading the AI adoption effort, ensuring that the benefits of AI are realized across all areas of the business.
3. **Create a Strategic Vision for AI Adoption:** The AI Change Team should develop a clear and compelling vision for how AI will be used in the organization. This vision should align with the organization›s overall strategy and goals. The AI Change Team at RetailCo develops an idea for how AI can transform their business. This includes using AI to personalize marketing campaigns, optimize inventory management, enhance customer service, and streamline supply chain operations.
4. **Communicate and Embed the AI Vision:** Once the vision is established, it needs to be communicated throughout the organization. The AI Change Team shares this vision with the entire organization. They hold town hall meetings, send

regular email updates, and incorporate AI-related goals into performance reviews. They also provide training sessions to help employees understand how AI will impact their roles and how they can contribute to the AI adoption effort.

5. **Overcome Barriers to AI Adoption:** Organizations will inevitably encounter barriers to AI adoption. These might include resistance from employees, technical challenges, or regulatory issues. The AI Change Team needs to anticipate these barriers and develop strategies to overcome them. RetailCo encounters several obstacles to AI adoption, including resistance from employees unfamiliar with AI and technical challenges related to data integration and privacy. The AI Change Team addresses these barriers by providing additional training, investing in necessary technology upgrades, and working with the legal and compliance team to ensure all AI initiatives adhere to data privacy regulations.

6. **Momentum with Quick Wins:** Quick wins are small, early successes demonstrating AI's value. They can help build momentum and support for AI adoption. To build momentum and demonstrate the value of AI, RetailCo started with a project to use AI to optimize inventory management. This project successfully reduced overstock and out-of-stock situations, leading to cost savings and improved customer satisfaction. This quick win builds enthusiasm and supports further AI initiatives.

7. **Maintain Continuous AI Momentum:** AI adoption is not a one-time project but an ongoing process. Organizations must continuously learn from their experiences, adjust their strategies, and pursue new AI initiatives. RetailCo understands that AI adoption is an ongoing journey. They constantly

monitor the performance of their AI initiatives, using the insights gained to improve their strategies and explore new AI projects. For example, after the success of the inventory management project, RetailCo decided to implement an AI-powered customer service chatbot.

8. **Anchor AI Adoption for Long-Term Success:** The final step is to ensure that AI becomes an integral part of the organization's operations and culture. This might involve updating policies and procedures, providing ongoing training, and celebrating AI successes. As AI initiatives become successful and more prevalent, RetailCo works to make AI an integral part of its operations and culture. They update their policies and procedures to incorporate AI tools, provide ongoing AI training sessions, and celebrate teams and individuals using AI effectively.

Each of these steps plays an essential role in the AI adoption process. They guide organizations through the complexities of AI integration, help them overcome potential obstacles, and ensure that AI adoption is not just a one-time project but a long-term strategic initiative. By following this model, organizations can navigate the path to AI success and maximize the benefits of AI adoption.

While we have mapped out the broader journey of AI adoption, the devil, as they say, is in the details. As we pivot to our next chapter, we will delve into the specifics of prompt engineering, AI tools, and APIs. These instruments fine-tune our AI symphony, ensuring precision in every note. So, as you turn the page, prepare to dive deeper into the art and science of AI, exploring the granular details that make the larger picture come alive.

QUICK GUIDE TO PROMPT ENGINEERING, AI TOOLS AND APIS

> *"The power to question is the basis of all human progress."*
> *– Indira Gandhi*

*I*n the ever-evolving business landscape, the ability to adapt and innovate is not just a luxury but a necessity. As we stand on the brink of the Fourth Industrial Revolution, powered by artificial intelligence, it's clear that the businesses that will thrive can harness AI's transformative power.

However, how can we, as business leaders, navigate this complex landscape and leverage AI to its full potential? This is the question that this chapter seeks to answer.

In the previous chapters, we have laid the groundwork, exploring the potential of AI and its implications for business and leadership. It's time to delve deeper and equip ourselves with the necessary practical skills and knowledge to navigate the AI landscape effectively. This chapter serves as a launchpad, a quick guide to the essential elements of working with AI: prompt engineering, understanding AI tools like ChatGPT, and leveraging APIs to automate your business workflow.

Prompt engineering is crafting practical instructions that guide AI tools like ChatGPT to generate the desired output. It's a crucial skill that can unlock the full potential of AI tools. On the other hand, understanding AI tools involves familiarizing ourselves with their capabilities and learning how to use them effectively. Lastly, APIs, or Application Programming Interfaces, are the bridges that allow different software systems to work together seamlessly, enabling us to create a streamlined, AI-powered workflow.

By mastering these elements, we can unlock the transformative power of AI and 10x our business and leadership impact. But remember, this chapter is not just about learning these skills; it's about understanding their significance in the larger context of our AI-powered future. It's about realizing that these skills are not just tools but keys to unlocking a world of possibilities.

The Power of Prompt Engineering

In the realm of artificial intelligence, communication is vital. How we interact with AI tools, particularly language models like ChatGPT and Google's Bard significantly influences their output. This interaction is facilitated through 'prompts,' instructions, or queries we provide to the AI. The art of effectively crafting these prompts is known as 'prompt engineering.' It's a skill that can unlock the full potential of artificial intelligence tools.

Prompt engineering is akin to having a conversation with the AI. The goal is to guide the AI to understand user requirements and deliver the best possible results. A well-crafted prompt can lead the AI to produce high-quality, relevant output. At the same time, a poorly designed one can result in off-topic or nonsensical responses.

Mastering prompt engineering involves:

- Understanding the mechanics of AI tools.
- Being specific with your instructions.
- Setting the proper context.
- Being willing to experiment and iterate.

It's a continuous learning and improvement process, but the rewards are worth the effort. Becoming proficient in prompt engineering allows you to leverage AI tools to 10x your business and leadership impact.

Prompt engineering is both an art and a science. It requires creativity, precision, and a willingness to iterate and improve. Here, I've outlined a step-by-step process to guide you through crafting the perfect prompts.

1. **Define Your Goal:** Start by identifying your goal. What do you want ChatGPT (or a similar Gen AI tool) to accomplish with its response?
2. **Set the Right Context:** Your prompt should give enough information to set the scene.
3. **Be Specific:** The more specific your prompt, the more likely the AI tool will generate the desired output.

4. **Experiment and Iterate:** Not all prompts yield perfect results the first time. Experiment with different phrasings, add more detail or clarify the context.
5. **Review and Refine:** Evaluate the generated output. If it didn't meet your goal, identify what went wrong, refine your prompt, and try again.

Mastering the Elements of a High-Quality Prompt

To craft an effective prompt, one needs to master several vital elements that go into it:

1. Context/Primer
2. Expert Persona
3. Initial Verbs
4. Length & Output Type
5. Specific Task and Objective
6. Tone of Voice
7. Target Audience
8. Purpose
9. Notes
10. Data and References

By understanding these elements and how to apply them effectively, you can craft high-quality prompts that align with your goals. Remember, these elements serve as a guide, and not every prompt will need all aspects. Use your judgment and experiment with different combinations to see what works best.

Practical Example of Crafting a High-Quality Prompt – 10-Step Magic Prompt

10 Step Magic Prompt Formula			
Step	Heading	Description	Example
1	Context/ Primer	Set the stage for the task, giving background information about the topic.	The skincare and wellness industry has seen significant growth with the rise of Ayurvedic luxury brands.
2	Expert Persona	Clarify the persona the AI should adopt to complete the task.	As a successful social media marketer…
3	Initial Verbs	Start the task with actionable verbs to guide the AI.	Develop a…
4	Specific Task and Objective	Exactly describe what the AI should do, specifying the goal of the task.	10-day social media content calendar for Divyaveda, a recently launched luxury Ayurveda brand, to improve engagement and click-through rates.

5	Length & Output Type	Indicate how extensive the response should be and the format it should be in.	Generate a detailed table that includes the day, type of content, outline, and any other elements that could boost post engagement.
6	Tone of Voice	Guide the AI on how to communicate the output.	Use a blend of casual and authoritative tones.
7	Target Audience	Specify who the content is meant for.	Appealing to fans of luxury, aspirational brands who are passionate about skincare and wellness.
8	Purpose	Explain why the AI is doing the task and what impact it should have.	The goal is to attract, engage, and inspire Divyaveda's social media followers, enhancing their brand experience.
9	Notes	Provide additional instructions that might help the AI better accomplish the task.	Make sure to include a mix of different types of content, like educational posts about Ayurveda, user-generated content, product promotions, and community engagement posts.

| 10 | Data and References | Mention any sources of inspiration or data the AI should consider while accomplishing the task. | Take inspiration from successful skincare brands like Forest Essentials and Biotique, particularly their high-engagement posts. Incorporate insights from studies on peak social media engagement times and strategies for the skincare industry. |

Final Prompt for CHATGPT - As a successful social media marketer, develop a 10-day social media content calendar for Divyaveda, a recently launched luxury Ayurveda brand, to improve engagement and click-through rates. Generate a detailed table that includes the day, type of content, outline, and any other elements that could boost post engagement. Use a blend of casual and authoritative tones, appealing to fans of luxury, aspirational brands who are passionate about skincare and wellness. The goal is to attract, engage, and inspire Divyaveda's social media followers, enhancing their brand experience. Make sure to include a mix of different types of content, like educational posts about Ayurveda, user-generated content, product promotions, and community engagement posts. Take inspiration from successful skincare brands like Forest Essentials and Biotique, particularly their high-engagement posts. Incorporate insights from studies on peak social media engagement times and strategies for the skincare industry.

CHATGPT Output:

Day	Type of Content	Brief Outline	Notes
Day 1	Educational Post	"Discover the ancient secrets of Ayurveda for radiant skin and a balanced mind. 🌿 Learn about the doshas and how they influence your skincare routine. #AyurvedaSkincare #DivyavedaBeauty"	Tip: Include a captivating image of Ayurvedic herbs or ingredients to enhance visual appeal.
Day 2	User-Generated Content	"Our community shares their love for Divyaveda! ♡ Share your skincare journey with us using #DivyavedaGlow for a chance to be featured! #SkincareCommunity"	Tip: Respond to user submissions with genuine appreciation and encourage more participation.

Day 3	Product Promotion	"Experience the ultimate luxury with our Ayurvedic skincare range! ❈ Indulge in natural ingredients and pure goodness. Shop now and get 20% off on your first purchase! #DivyavedaLuxury #AyurvedicBeauty"	Tip: Highlight customer reviews or testimonials to build trust and credibility.
Day 4	Community Engagement	"We believe in the power of self-care and wellness. 🧖 Share your favorite self-care routine and tag a friend who deserves some pampering! #SelfCareSunday #WellnessWednesday"	Tip: Run a self-care challenge and encourage followers to share their routines throughout the week.
Day 5	High-Engagement Post	"🌸 Embrace the goodness of nature with Divyaveda's floral-infused skincare. Which flower is your favorite? Comment below and let us know! #FloralSkincare #DivyavedaFlowers"	Tip: Use emojis to add personality and make the post visually appealing.

Day 6	Educational Post	"Did you know that Gua Sha has been used in Ayurvedic skincare for centuries? Learn how to use this ancient beauty tool for glowing skin! #GuaShaBeauty #AyurvedaSecrets"	Tip: Create a short video tutorial demonstrating Gua Sha techniques for better engagement.
Day 7	User-Generated Content	"Our community's selfies speak volumes about their love for Divyaveda! 📷 Share your skincare selfies with #DivyavedaSelfie and join the glowing community! #SkincareAddict"	Tip: Share some user-submitted selfies in your Instagram Stories to encourage more submissions.
Day 8	Product Promotion	"Treat yourself to a spa-like experience at home with Divyaveda's Ayurvedic face masks! 🧖 Shop now and get a free handmade headband with your purchase! #SpaAtHome #DivyavedaMasks"	Tip: Use Instagram Reels to showcase the application of face masks and the relaxing experience.

Day 9	Community Engagement	"Spread positivity and love with a compliment! 💬 Tag a friend and compliment them to brighten their day. #ComplimentYour Friend #PositiveVibes Only"	Tip: Respond to comments with positive affirmations and engage in conversations with your followers.
Day 10	High-Engagement Post	"Our journey to natural radiance starts with self-love and care. 💖 Share your favorite self-love quote and inspire others to embrace their unique beauty! #SelfLove Quotes #Divyaveda Love"	Tip: Pair the quote with an aesthetically pleasing image that aligns with Divyaveda's branding.

This is just a basic output to introduce you to the power of prompt engineering. I recommend you test it out for your own business or leadership use case and let the magic unfold.

With these tools and insights, you're now ready to embark on your journey to become an effective prompt engineer. Remember, the key is to continuously learn, experiment, and iterate. Happy prompting!

An Introduction to AI Tools

The next step in our journey is understanding the AI tools at your disposal. ChatGPT, Google's Bard, and Bing are powerful AI tools that can be the foundation of your AI-powered business strategy.

ChatGPT is a language model developed by OpenAI that can generate creative, coherent, and contextually relevant text. It's a versatile tool that can be used for various tasks, from drafting emails and writing code to brainstorming ideas and tutoring in multiple subjects. With a dedicated plugin store and new capabilities like Code Interpreter being rolled out, ChatGPT 4 has turned into a powerhouse for almost every business use case.

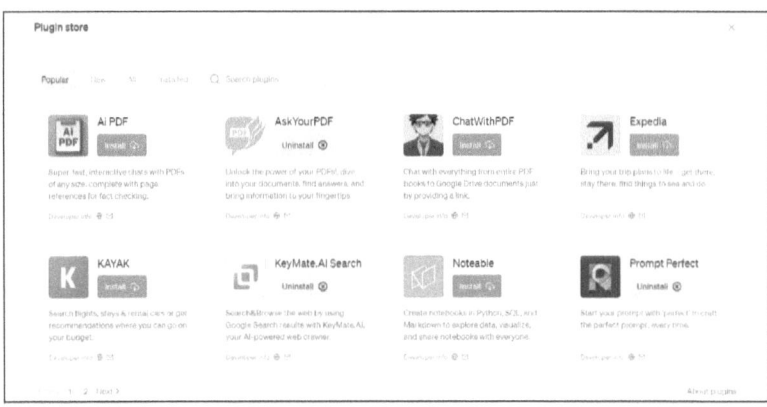

Figure 9 - ChatGPT Plugin Store (Source – ChatGPT)

Then, there's Google's Bard and Microsoft Bing, which exemplify advancements in natural language processing and address the limitation of ChatGPT in terms of live searches. New AI tools emerge daily, catering to diverse business use cases. By understanding the capabilities of these tools and how to use them effectively, you can cover a wide range of use cases and significantly enhance your business operations.

AI technology isn't just limited to language models like ChatGPT or Google's Bard. Numerous AI tools have been developed, each with unique functionality and use cases. They can be used with language models, offering many possibilities.

As we delve into AI, we'll discover how these powerful tools can supercharge your business and leadership impact, propelling you toward unprecedented growth and success.

To give a glimpse into this expansive world:

- Dall-E 2 transforms text prompts into computer graphics.
- Lumen5 offers an AI-powered video creation tool that is ideal for marketing content.
- Looka uses AI to design unique logos, simplifying branding efforts.
- Podcastle integrates AI tools for audio recording, ensuring professional-sounding outputs.
- Legal Robot translates complex legal jargon into understandable language, bridging the gap between legal professionals and laymen.
- Cleanup.Pictures uses AI for image retouching, ensuring perfection in every shot.

And the list goes on. From automating note-taking in meetings with Fireflies to ensuring clear communication in conference calls with Krisp, AI tools are becoming indispensable.

In conclusion, as AI continues its upward trajectory, it's crucial for businesses and individuals to familiarize themselves with these tools. Beyond the well-known applications like ChatGPT, Google Bard, and Microsoft Bing, there exists a vast array of AI tools designed to optimize every facet of business and leadership.

Check out this sample list of 50 AI tools and discover the transformative power they hold for businesses:

Number	Tool	Business Area	Description of Tool
1	Bubble	App Development	Create powerful apps with no code
2	Speechify	Audio	AI tool to convert text to Audio
3	Adobe Podcast	Audio	AI-powered audio tools that elevate your voice
4	Murf	Audio	Text-to-speech engine creating natural-sounding vocal recordings in multiple languages.
5	UiPath	Automation	AI-powered platform for automating repetitive business processes.

6	Zapier	Automation	Automate the entire business by connecting Apps via Zaps
7	Looka	Branding & Design	AI tool for logo creation, aligning with company style and messaging.
8	Apollo io	Business Development	AI tool for lead generation
9	Sendspark	Business Development	AI tool to send personalized videos
10	Krisp	Communication	Removes background noises in real-time during conference calls.
11	Poised AI Tool	Communication	AI tool for improving public speaking skills and communication coach

12	Jasper	Content Creation	AI tool for generating articles, ads, and other written content.
13	Shakespeare AI	Content Creation	AI-driven writing assistant for various content needs.
14	Quillbot	Content Creation	Enhances your writing and boosts your productivity anywhere online
15	Zoho's Zia	CRM & Sales	AI-driven sales assistant for Zoho's CRM platform, providing insights and automation.
16	Botpress	Customer Support	AI-powered chat interfaces that provide real-time customer support, answering queries and guiding users.

17	H2O	Data Analysis	Data analysis & reporting platform for businesses.
18	IBM Watson	Data Analysis	AI tool for data analysis, insights generation, and more.
19	ScraperAPI	Data Extraction	AI tool for efficient web scraping.
20	Tableau's AI	Data Visualization	AI-driven data visualization tools that provide insights and predictive analytics.
21	SkyMind	Deep Learning	Offers a suite of tools and solutions for building and deploying deep learning in commercial applications.

22	Midjourney	Design	Transforms text prompts into computer graphics, including images, photos, and drawings.
23	Affectiva	Emotion Recognition	Uses AI to analyze human emotions and reactions through facial expressions and voice.
24	Kasisto	Financial Services	Provides conversational AI for the finance industry.
25	Zavvy	HR & Recruitment	AI tool for human resource management
26	Adobe FireFly	Image Creation	AI tool to create Images, videos and more
27	Canva AI	Image Creation	AI tool to create Images, videos and more
28	Clio	Legal	AI tool for legal department

29	TensorFlow	Machine Learning	Open-source platform that helps businesses build and deploy ML models.
30	Voluum	Marketing	AI-driven platform for affiliate marketing.
31	AB Testing AI	Marketing	AI-powered A/B testing tool to optimize marketing campaigns.
32	Fireflies	Meeting Assistance	Automates note-taking and transcription during video conferences, providing insights into conversations.
33	OtterAI	Meeting Assistance	AI tool for meeting notes and summaries.

34	Replika	Mental Well-being	AI companion chatbot designed to engage in text-based conversations and provide emotional support.
35	Soundraw	Music & Audio	Automated music generator that creates royalty-free AI music based on user preferences.
36	Cleanup.Pictures	Photography	AI tool for image retouching and removing unwanted objects or imperfections.
37	Gamma App	Presentation	Create compelling presentations at the click of a button
38	Humata	Productivity	Ask questions and get answers about any file Instantly

39	Typewise	Productivity	AI tool for boosting productivity in writing.
40	Wondershare	Productivity	Brainstorming and mindmaps with AI
41	Trello's AI	Project Management	AI enhancements for Trello's project management tool, providing insights and automation.
42	Surfer	SEO	AI tool for SEO and content optimization.
43	Formula Dog	Spreadsheet Management	AI tool for generating Excel formulas and spotting errors.
44	Lumen5	Video Creation	AI-powered video creation tool with a drag-and-drop interface.
45	Pictory	Video Creation	AI-driven platform for video content creation.

46	Synthesia	Video Creation	AI tool for creating unique video content.
47	Framer AI	Web Development	Create website with no code
48	Uizard	Web Development	Design stunning mockup for your web or app in minutes
49	ScribeHow	Workflow	AI tool for creating step-by-step guides from screen recordings.
50	Grammarly	Writing & Editing	AI-powered writing assistant that provides real-time grammar and style corrections.

Remember, the goal of this book is not just to introduce you to these tools. I aim to provide you with a process, a launchpad, that will enable you to harness the power of AI in your business and leadership journey. You can use more sophisticated tools as you progress, adapt to the evolving AI landscape, and continue to 10x your impact.

APIs: The Key to Automating Your Business Workflow

Another important part of our toolkit is understanding the role of APIs in automating business workflows. APIs, or Application Programming Interfaces, are sets of rules and protocols that allow different software applications to communicate with each other. They serve as bridges between different software systems, enabling them to work together seamlessly.

For instance, the ChatGPT API allows your business software to interact with the ChatGPT model. This means you can integrate ChatGPT's capabilities into your existing systems, customizing its usage to suit your needs.

By using APIs, you can automate various processes, enhance efficiency, and drive innovation. They allow you to create a seamless, AI-powered workflow where different tools work together to achieve your business goals.

In conclusion, mastering prompt engineering, understanding the capabilities of essential AI tools, and leveraging APIs to automate your business workflow are crucial steps in harnessing the power of AI. By mastering these skills, you can unlock the full potential of AI tools and 10x your business and leadership impact. The journey may be challenging, but the rewards are worth the effort. So, let's dive in and embark on this exciting journey together!

So, are you ready to dive into AI and transform your business? In the upcoming sections, we will dive into ten plug-and-play AI-driven strategies to 10x your leadership and business impact. Let us embark on this exciting journey together!

BE THE 10X LEADER: UNLOCK YOUR LEADERSHIP POTENTIAL WITH AI

"The task of leadership is not to put greatness into people, but to elicit it, for the greatness is there already."
– John Buchan

*I*n the bustling city of Techville, where innovation and ambition collided, Alex Turner led the charge as the CEO of Luminary Technologies, a fast-growing tech startup. With each passing day, the challenges of steering his company toward success increased, demanding an extraordinary approach to leadership. Alex knew he had to level up his game and become a 10x leader—an unparalleled force that could revolutionize the industry and inspire his team to reach new heights.

Like Tony Stark and his trusty AI companion, JARVIS, Alex found his futuristic ally in LUMI. This AI-powered assistant was more than just a program—it was a catalyst for transformation.

As the sun dawned on another day of possibilities, Alex's journey as a 10x leader with the aid of AI was about to unfold.

A Day in the Life of Alex Turner: Embracing the Leadership Challenge

The morning sun streamed through the windows of Alex's contemporary loft apartment, marking the beginning of a new day filled with possibilities. As he stepped into his home office, he was greeted by LUMI, the AI-powered assistant that had become an indispensable part of his daily routine.

"Good morning, Alex," LUMI chimed. "Today is going to be an adventurous journey of growth and success. Let's get started!"

1. Mastering the Juggling Act: Multitasking

Alex's day kicked off with a virtual team meeting. As he joined the conference call, LUMI efficiently managed the technical aspects with the help of **OTTER AI**, which took meeting notes and provided a concise summary. This ensured a seamless start to the discussion. However, Alex's inbox overflowed with emails as the meeting progressed, pulling his attention in multiple directions.

"LUMI, I need your help to manage my inbox. Prioritize the urgent ones and set reminders for the rest," Alex requested.

Without hesitation, LUMI utilized **RightInbox**, a powerful tool that could prioritize emails, set follow-ups, create templates, track emails, and more. It swiftly sorted through the messages, allowing Alex to focus on the meeting with his team. With LUMI as his personal productivity ally, Alex confidently juggled the demands of being a CEO, providing valuable insights to his team while staying on top of his communication.

2. The Art of Captivating Storytelling: Effective Presentations

Later in the day, Alex prepared for a crucial presentation to potential investors. As he worked on his slides, he couldn't shake the feeling that the content lacked that spark to captivate his audience.

"LUMI, I need this presentation to be compelling. Can you help me find data insights that will strengthen my narrative?" Alex asked.

LUMI swiftly analyzed vast market data using the **CHATGPT Code Interpreter**, a master data scientist, to extract relevant trends and patterns. It then utilized the **Gamma App**, which effortlessly created a presentation with the content at the click of a button and masterfully crafted speaker notes with the help of CHATGPT, which Alex could refine further with minimal effort.

With data-backed insights and visually stunning graphics, the presentation became a powerful story that impressed the investors and instilled confidence in the Luminary Technologies vision.

3. Commanding the Helm: Data Management, Planning, and Decision Making

Throughout the day, Alex faced several critical decisions that would shape the future of Luminary Technologies. His desk's sheer volume of data was overwhelming, and he knew that data-driven decisions were essential for success.

"LUMI, I need your assistance in processing and analyzing this data. Help me make informed decisions," Alex requested.

LUMI diligently analyzed the data using the **Akkio** tool, providing real-time feedback and insights, predicting business metrics like revenue, costs, and market trends, and identifying the best leads to pursue. This gave Luminary Technologies a competitive edge in planning and strategy formulation.

4. Star-Gazing: Staying Updated with Industry Developments and Customer Trends

Alex recognized the importance of staying informed about industry developments as the day progressed. Being caught off guard in the fast-paced tech world could harm Luminary Technologies' growth.

"LUMI, keep an eye on the industry for emerging trends, competitor moves, and relevant news. I want to be ahead of the game," Alex instructed.

LUMI diligently monitored market research reports, analyzed news articles with the help of **Feedly AI**, which picked the most important news, summarized vital points using **ChatGPT**, and sent a message to Alex with crucial updates—all automated with **Zapier**. Additionally, LUMI leveraged **Brandwatch** to analyze real-time customer feedback and competitive insights. LUMI even used **Humata** to quickly summarize 5 recently concluded earning call reports of key competitors. With LUMI as his telescope to the cosmos of the tech industry, Alex felt confident in steering Luminary Technologies in the right direction.

5. Stellar Impact: Boosting Your Industry Influence

As Alex reviewed Luminary Technologies' accomplishments and aspirations, he pondered the company's industry influence. To be a true 10x leader, he wanted Luminary Technologies to be a thought leader, setting standards and influencing industry trends. Alex had a virtual tech industry conference to attend in the hour as a panelist and needed to prep for it amidst all the juggling.

"LUMI, how can I prepare for the conference and deliver an impactful narrative? What topics should I focus on?" Alex inquired.

LUMI swiftly researched using **Microsoft Bing** to provide valuable insights into hot topics and emerging trends that Alex could address. It then used **Jasper AI's** writing capabilities to craft high-quality, industry-specific content that positioned Alex and Luminary Technologies as thought leaders in the conference. With LUMI's support, Alex's influence in the tech industry grew exponentially.

6. Discover New Horizons: Enhancing Creativity and Innovation with AI

As the day ventured into late afternoon, Alex focused on fostering creativity and innovation within his team. Luminary Technologies' success depended on pushing the boundaries and thinking outside the box.

"LUMI, inspire my team with fresh ideas and innovative solutions. Help us lead the way in technological advancements," Alex requested.

LUMI employed machine learning algorithms to analyze vast data, presenting the team with unique insights and groundbreaking solutions. As Alex needed to work on the Luminary Technologies app and brief his product and design agency, Lumi quickly pulled out **Figma** to help Alex translate his thoughts into a compelling flowchart. Then, the **Bubble io** app helped Alex create a prototype to bring his vision to reality with fewer to-and-fro discussions and help Alex move fast.

7. Mapping the Stars Together: Collaboration Made Easier with AI

As the evening approached, Alex acknowledged the importance of seamless collaboration among his team members. He understood teamwork was essential to charting Luminary Technologies' path to success.

"LUMI, improve our team's collaboration and communication. Help us navigate through challenges together," Alex said.

LUMI analyzed team messages, suggesting improvements for better clarity and understanding. It efficiently allocated tasks based on individual skills and tracked real-time progress. With LUMI as their reliable navigator, the Luminary Technologies team worked harmoniously, achieving their goals precisely. Additionally, LUMI pulled up **Notion** to help Alex project manage all key work initiatives, ensuring seamless collaboration and effective communication within the team.

8. Building and Engaging the Team: AI

As the day inched to a close, Alex faced numerous tasks and competing priorities. Whether recruiting or engaging the team, having the right and engaged talent was critical to his company's success.

"LUMI, help me find the right and engaged talent. I need to stay focused on what truly matters," Alex urged.

LUMI quickly pulled out **TalentGPT** and a few other tools from its arsenal to draft job descriptions and set up a process to conduct initial CV and video screening. It also used the **Happily AI** tool to send timely team surveys, spot opportunities, and identify areas for improvement.

With LUMI as his intelligent navigation system, Alex was empowered to navigate the cosmic storm of leadership with grace, clarity, and a supercharged 10x team.

9. Stellar Evolution: Self-Growth and Development with AI

As the day at work was about to end, Alex recognized the significance of continuous self-improvement. To be a 10x leader, he needed to evolve and grow alongside his company.

"LUMI, guide me on my journey of personal development. Recommend courses and resources for my growth and help me deliver my narrative effectively," Alex requested.

LUMI became Alex's astronomical observatory, curating a personalized learning experience for Alex with AI learning tools aligned with his interests and aspirations. It monitored his progress, provided real-time feedback, and adapted learning recommendations based on his growth journey. LUMI even pulled out **Yoodli AI** as a personal speech coach to help Alex improve in using power words, inclusivity, and other aspects of speech.

10. AI as the 10x Support System Round the Clock

As the night sky adorned the cityscape with stars, Alex couldn't help but marvel at the day's achievements. He owed much of his success to LUMI, his ever-reliable executive assistant and coach.

"LUMI, thank you for being my constant companion throughout this cosmic journey. You've been invaluable as you helped me accomplish 10 times more than what I could have done on my own," Alex expressed his gratitude.

LUMI beamed with virtual satisfaction. "It has been my honor to support you, Alex. Our journey together has just begun, and I am excited for the future."

As Alex prepared for the next day's cosmic voyage, he knew that the AI revolution had transformed him into a 10x leader. With LUMI by his side, he was equipped to lead Luminary Technologies to new frontiers of success. The possibilities were infinite, and the journey ahead was filled with opportunities to explore the uncharted territories of the tech industry.

Alex's determination burned brightly as the city's lights dimmed, eager to embrace the cosmic challenges that awaited him and Luminary Technologies. Together with AI, Alex was confident in reaching for the stars and beyond, realizing that the future of leadership was limitless.

KEY PLUG-N-PLAY STRATEGIES FOR AI APPLICATION IN BUSINESS – AN INTRODUCTION

"The best time to plant a tree was 20 years ago. The second best time is now."
— *Chinese Proverb*

*I*n this section, we continue our saga, where we have unlocked our true potential and transformed into a 10x version of ourselves. As you embrace the power of AI, you realize its transformative force that can revolutionize every facet of your business.

As you embark on your entrepreneurial journey, imagine yourself as the founder of a fast-growing startup fueled by determination and dreams of conquering new frontiers in the business universe. You are not alone in this cosmic voyage; your trusted AI co-pilot stands beside you, equipped with unparalleled intelligence and capabilities to amplify your every move.

Before we delve into how AI can revolutionize various aspects of your business, let's equip you with a simple toolkit to understand when and how to apply AI effectively so you can think along these lines as we explore examples of AI applications.

The Simple Rule to Apply AI

Think of this rule as a treasure map, leading you to the perfect spot to bury your AI 'seed' for maximum growth. This spot is where three essential conditions meet:

1. **Repetitive and Rule-Based Tasks:** These tasks follow a set pattern and must be performed consistently. Imagine a task that›s like a song on repeat—it's the same rhythm and melody repeatedly. AI loves this kind of music!
2. **Abundant High-Quality Data:** AI thrives on data. It›s like the water and sunlight that a seed needs to grow. The more high-quality data you have, the better AI can learn and perform.
3. **High Value or Impact Tasks:** These are tasks that, when performed well, can significantly impact your business. It›s like planting your seed where the grown tree will provide the most shade.

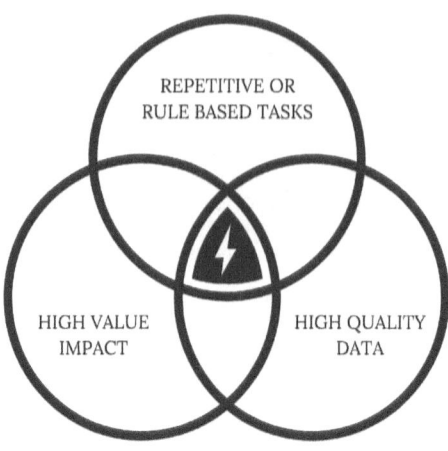

Figure 10 - Simple AI Application Rule For Business

Where these three conditions meet is the sweet spot for AI applications. It's the perfect place to plant your AI seed and watch it grow into a thriving tree.

AI Application Framework - IDEA (Ideate, Develop, Execute, Adapt)

Let's think of the IDEA method as a journey, a roadmap to successfully implementing AI in your business:

1. **Ideate:** This is the first step of your journey, where you look at the landscape of your business and identify where AI can make a difference. It›s like spotting a piece of land where a new tree could provide much-needed shade. For example, you might identify that your customer support team is overwhelmed with inquiries, and an AI chatbot could help manage the load.
2. **Develop:** Now that you›ve identified where to plant your AI ‹seed,› it›s time to prepare it for planting. This could involve

training a machine learning model with relevant data like a farmer nurturing a seedling and preparing it for planting. For instance, you might feed your AI chatbot with data from previous customer interactions so it can learn how to respond effectively.

3. **Execute:** It›s planting time! You implement the AI solution in your business operations and watch it grow. But your job is ongoing—you must monitor its growth and performance, just like a farmer watches over his growing plants. For example, you might track how well your AI chatbot handles customer inquiries and whether it's improving response times.

4. **Adapt:** Just like a farmer adjusts his care based on how the plant is growing, you need to make necessary adjustments to your AI solution based on feedback and performance. This could involve re-training the model with more data or tweaking its parameters to improve performance. For instance, if your AI chatbot is struggling with specific inquiries, you should provide more training data related to those inquiries.

This journey doesn't end here. The world of AI is constantly evolving, and so should your AI solutions. Keep exploring, learning, and adapting, and watch your 'AI tree' grow and flourish.

Join me as I guide you through the boundless possibilities of AI in optimizing market research, amplifying branding and marketing efforts, streamlining sales and business development, and enhancing the overall customer experience. Together, we will unleash the true potential of AI in finance, HR, project management, and more, turning your company into a cosmic cruiser destined for greatness.

Let's take a sneak peek into the chapters that follow:

Chapter 7: AI and the Future of Market Research & Product Development

In market research and product development, AI-powered tools analyze vast customer data, uncovering deep insights into customer preferences, pain points, and emerging trends. This enables informed decisions about product innovation and development, delivering products that truly resonate with the target audience and gaining a competitive edge in the market.

Chapter 8: Branding and Marketing: Supercharged by AI

AI-driven algorithms analyze customer behavior and engagement data, guiding the crafting of personalized marketing campaigns. The company's social media presence is optimized through AI-powered analytics, resulting in higher customer engagement and increased brand loyalty. Stellar branding and marketing become critical drivers of business growth.

Chapter 9: Amplify Your Sales and Business Development with AI

Sales and business development see a significant boost with AI integration. AI-powered sales automation tools prioritize leads and streamline the sales process. AI-driven chatbots engage with potential customers, addressing queries promptly and improving conversion rates. The sales team can now focus on building meaningful client relationships, resulting in increased customer satisfaction and more significant business opportunities.

Chapter 10: AI-Driven Strategy, Planning, and Analytics

As the company expands, data complexity increases. But fear not! With AI-driven analytics and planning, insights into market dynamics and competitor strategies are gained. AI predicts potential roadblocks and suggests optimal business strategies. This data-driven decision-making empowers the company to lead with confidence and agility, setting them on a sustainable growth path.

Chapter 11: AI and the Transformation of Supply Chain Management

Supply chain management becomes a seamless operation with AI integration. AI-driven logistics systems optimize inventory management, predicting demand patterns and ensuring timely deliveries. The company now operates like a well-oiled machine, minimizing costs and enhancing customer satisfaction.

Chapter 12: Revolutionizing Customer Experience and Support with AI

Exceptional customer experience has become the company's hallmark, thanks to AI. AI-powered chatbots and virtual assistants provide 24/7 support, catering to customer needs round-the-clock. Sentiment analysis through AI enables proactive response to customer feedback, further enhancing loyalty and advocacy.

Chapter 13: The AI-Driven Business Process Automation

Internal operations are streamlined with AI-driven business process automation. AI systems now efficiently handle repetitive tasks, freeing up the team's time for strategic initiatives and innovation. The company becomes more agile and adaptable, outperforming competitors in efficiency and productivity.

Chapter 14: HR, Learning, Development, and Recruitment in the Age of AI

AI-driven HR tools revolutionize talent acquisition and development. AI-powered applicant screening shortlists the most suitable candidates, and AI-driven learning platforms facilitate employee growth and upskilling. The company has become an attractive workplace for top talent, institutionalizing a culture of continuous learning and development.

Chapter 15: Going Digital: AI and Your Web, App, Social Media Strategy

AI is embraced to optimize the digital presence. AI-driven algorithms personalize web and app interfaces, ensuring a seamless and engaging user experience. Social media strategies are enhanced with AI analytics, driving higher user engagement and expanding the company's digital footprint.

Chapter 16: Beyond the Obvious: AI in Finance, Legal, Project Management, and More

AI is harnessed in finance, legal, and project management. AI-powered financial analysis aids in resource allocation and budget optimization. Legal processes become more efficient with AI's contract review capabilities. Project management benefits from AI's predictive insights, ensuring timely project completion.

As we begin this incredible journey, I encourage you to move forward with the understanding that the potential of AI is at your fingertips. The upcoming sections will act as your practical guidebook, providing valuable advice and support on utilizing AI in all areas of your business.

HARNESSING AI TO REVOLUTIONIZE MARKET RESEARCH & PRODUCT DEVELOPMENT

"If I had asked people what they wanted, they would have said faster horses."
– Henry Ford

A couple of years ago, I found myself navigating the uncharted territory of launching a new product in the baby cologne category. Teamed up with my marketing head, we plunged deep into the world of our customers. Our mission was to decode their needs, wants, and desires.

We found ourselves in living rooms, poring over survey forms, listening to the heartfelt stories of hundreds of consumers. We aimed to capture their essence and decipher the code hidden in their daily routines, product usage, unmet needs, and aspirational values.

Each interview and conversation provided a piece of the puzzle. It was satisfying, yes, but I also felt the clock ticking. Time was precious, and the process was painstakingly slow. The wealth of information had to be synthesized, patterns needed to be identified, and insights extracted.

Then came the equally exhaustive task of translating these insights into tangible products. Collaborating with the research and development team, we juggled possible ingredients, fragrances, and unique selling propositions. It was a ballet of sourcing raw materials, figuring out packaging, and more.

Finally, our baby was ready for its first introduction to the world. But even then, our journey was far from over. Next up were customer tests, product tweaks, and multiple iterations, each demanding a fair share of time and effort.

As I reflected on my journey, it was evident that time was a precious commodity we cannot waste in today's competitive world. The speed of changing customer preferences is unforgiving, and we must keep up as leaders and business owners.

That's when it struck me. There was a need for a tool to transform this mammoth task into an agile, efficient process—a device that could quicken our steps and enrich the path with deeper insights and actionable intelligence. And that's when I found artificial intelligence, the game changer!

In this section, I'll walk you through the fascinating world of AI, its power to revolutionize market research and product development, and how you can harness this 10x power for your business. Let us dive in!

The Conventional Approach

In the past, market research followed a more straightforward, almost quaint process. Businesses rolled out surveys with carefully framed questions, and statisticians crunched the numbers to make sense of the consumer pulse. Yet, as the market became a hotbed of competition and consumer tastes twisted and turned into complex patterns, the lens shifted toward a more qualitative form of research. This new wave sought to unravel the tangled web of motivations, emotions, and hidden desires that guide consumer behavior.

Yet, like all things, this conventional approach came with its share of imperfections:

Time is of the Essence: Traditional research is akin to a slow-cooked meal, where each stage, from drafting surveys to deciphering responses, takes its own sweet time to come together. But in today's fast-paced market, every moment counts, and this lengthy process can sometimes feel like a drawn-out chess game where the rules keep changing.

Scope, So Limited: The reach of these traditional techniques stretches only so far, bound by the trammels of resources, time, and accessibility. In a world that's getting smaller every day, this restricted view can often leave blind spots in understanding the diverse consumer landscape.

The Subjectivity Pitfall: Qualitative research, focusing on human emotions and motivations, is a mighty sword in the modern business arsenal. But wielded poorly, it's prone to subjectivity, opening doors to potential bias and skewed conclusions.

The Data Deluge: The flood of unstructured data pouring in from various channels, be it focus groups, interviews, or the chaotic world of social media, often leaves businesses knee-deep in information with no apparent way out. Analyzing and deriving meaning from this tidal wave of data can be overwhelming.

These challenges in traditional market research underscore the need for a new hero in this narrative—one that can deliver speed, efficiency, and precision without compromises. Enter

artificial intelligence. Equipped with the power to overcome these hurdles, AI is set to rewrite the rules of market research. Now, let's dive deeper into how this transformation takes shape.

AI as the Game-Changer: Transforming Market Research & Product Development

AI has become an integral part of the present-day business landscape. Its power to analyze and understand vast volumes of data is redefining market research in more ways than one:

Predictive Analytics: One of the most revolutionary contributions of AI to market research is its predictive capabilities. Machine learning algorithms can analyze past trends, behaviors, and data patterns to predict future events. These predictions can significantly influence strategic decisions around product development, marketing initiatives, and customer engagement strategies. Imagine knowing the potential demand for a product even before it hits the market or understanding how a change in pricing can influence future sales; that's the power of AI's predictive analytics!

Automation: Market research involves numerous repetitive and time-consuming tasks. Cleaning and organizing data, coding responses, translation, managing databases—the list goes on. AI can automate these tasks, speeding up the research process and freeing researchers to focus on what matters—interpreting results and formulating actionable insights. This not only saves time but also reduces human error and enhances the accuracy of the research.

Supercharged Qualitative Research: Traditional qualitative research methods like interviews and focus groups are limited, often failing to capture the complete picture of consumers' emotions and subconscious responses. AI is pushing these boundaries. Tools like facial coding can detect even the slightest changes in a consumer's facial expression, revealing their emotional reaction to a product or service. Sentiment analysis can help understand consumers' attitudes and emotions from their written or spoken language. Voice AI can analyze speech patterns and tones to provide deeper insights into consumer behavior.

Real-time Insights: In a world where trends and consumer preferences change overnight, businesses need real-time data to stay ahead. AI can provide this. It can analyze social media feeds, online reviews, and other real-time data sources to provide up-to-the-minute consumer sentiment and behavior insights and enable businesses to respond to changes more quickly and effectively.

Crafting Customer Personas: AI simplifies the creation of customer personas—detailed profiles of your ideal customer. AI can quickly develop nuanced personas by rapidly analyzing demographics, buying behavior, and online interactions. These AI-driven profiles, updated dynamically as new data rolls in, help businesses better understand their customers' needs and enhance their marketing and product development strategies.

Personalization: With AI, businesses can analyze consumer behavior and purchase history to create personalized products and recommendations and elevate user experience. This level of personalization can enhance customer engagement and loyalty.

AI is a powerful tool for market research and product development. But it's not just about having the right tools; it's also about knowing how to use them effectively. Let us look at how some industry leaders use AI to boost their market research and product development.

Real-Life Examples
Starbucks unlocking the power of AI

Imagine this: you stroll into your favorite Starbucks. The aroma of freshly ground coffee lures you in, and baristas greet you with a familiar smile, perhaps even remembering your go-to order. Yet, as you sip your meticulously crafted latte, there's something extraordinary brewing beneath this comforting scene.

Invisible yet instrumental, Starbucks' AI platform "Deep Brew" works quietly behind the counter. It starts its magic even before you set foot in the store. Every time you use the Starbucks mobile app to pre-order your drink, Deep Brew learns more about you—your preferred beverage, frequent store location, and even your usual order time.

And as you step into the store, a new drink suggestion pops up on your app. This isn't a random guess but a carefully tailored recommendation, brewed to your unique taste and preferences. It may be a seasonal special or a novel creation, resulting from Deep Brew analyzing customers' tastes and preferences to help Starbucks craft an irresistible menu.

Have you ever marveled at how a Starbucks store always seems to be conveniently nearby? That's Deep Brew's work, too. It gleans through data on local demographics, traffic patterns, and competitor presence to determine the best location for each new Starbucks store.

The next time you walk into Starbucks, remember it's not just your coffee shop crafting your coffee experience; it's a fascinating blend of technology and tradition, a dance of coffee beans and data bytes, a testament to the incredible power of AI in enhancing our daily experiences.

AstraZeneca

In the realm of healthcare, the application of AI is revolutionizing the way we approach drug development. AstraZeneca, a leading pharmaceutical company, is at the forefront of this transformation. The company is leveraging AI to expedite drug development, making the process faster and more cost-effective. The technology is used to mine vast archives of scientific reports, including gene sequences and academic papers, to identify promising drug targets. This approach has already yielded potential targets that human researchers might have overlooked.

The innovation doesn't stop at target identification. AstraZeneca also uses AI to design drug molecules that interact effectively with these targets. The company harnesses machine learning to sift through vast pools of potential drug molecules, predicting how they might behave in the body. This allows many early experiments to be carried out in silico, reducing the need for time-consuming lab work.

Their ultimate goal is to create more effective drugs with fewer side effects, improving patient outcomes. This AI-driven approach to drug development is not only transforming AstraZeneca's operations but also setting a new standard for the pharmaceutical industry.

Integrating AI into Market Research and Product Development

The application of AI can revolutionize the way market research and product development are conducted. Here's a step-by-step guide on how to integrate AI at each stage to create a robust strategy:

- **Identifying Market Trends:** AI tools like Brandwatch can help you identify emerging trends in your market. By analyzing massive amounts of data from various sources, these tools can provide insights into consumer behavior, preferences, and needs, helping you stay ahead of the curve.
- **Competitor Analysis:** AI can streamline the process of competitor analysis. Tools like SEMRush use AI to analyze

your competitors' online activities, providing insights into their SEO strategies, advertising campaigns, and more. This lets you understand their strengths and weaknesses and develop strategies to gain a competitive edge.

- **Customer Segmentation:** AI can enhance the accuracy and efficiency of customer segmentation. Tools like Hubspot use machine learning algorithms to analyze customer data and segment them based on various factors such as demographics, behavior, and customer preferences, allowing you to tailor your marketing and product strategies to meet the specific needs of each segment.
- **Product Ideation:** AI can assist in the product ideation process. Tools like Zeda analyze customer feedback, reviews, and queries, providing insights into customers' wants or needs. This can inspire new product ideas that align with customer needs.
- **Product Design:** AI can streamline the product design process. Tools like Midjourney use AI to generate multiple design options based on your specifications. You can choose the design which meets your needs, saving time and resources.
- **Prototype Testing:** AI can enhance the efficiency of prototype testing. Tools like UserTesting use AI to gather and analyze user feedback on your prototypes, providing insights into their usability and appeal and allowing you to refine your product before it hits the market.
- **Product Launch:** AI can optimize your product launch strategy. Tools like Marketo use AI to analyze past launch data and suggest the best timing, promotional strategy, and target audience for your new product. This ensures that your product makes a splash when it hits the market.

- **Post-Launch Analysis:** AI can provide valuable insights into your product's performance post-launch. Tools like Tableau use AI to analyze sales data, customer feedback, and other relevant data, providing insights into how well your product is performing and where improvements can be made.

Integrating AI into each step of your market research and product development process allows you to gain deeper insights, streamline operations, and create products that truly resonate with your target audience. It's about combining the power of AI with human creativity and strategic thinking to develop products that meet customer needs and stand out in the market.

AI-Powered Market Research and Product Development

Stage Name	Stage Description	What Happens	How AI Can Help	Example AI Tools
Niche Identification	Market Research Stage	Identification of potential market niches for a product or service	AI can analyze vast amounts of data to identify trends, preferences, and potential market niches	Ideas AI, Nichely AI
Customer Segmentation	Market Segmentation Stage	Segmentation of potential customers into distinct groups based on various factors	AI can analyze customer data to create detailed and accurate customer segments	HubSpot, Salesforce Einstein

	Stage	Description	AI Application	Tools
Persona Development	Customer Understanding Stage	Development of detailed customer personas based on market research	AI can analyze customer behavior and preferences to create detailed and accurate customer personas	Crystal Knows, Delve AI
Competitor Scraping	Competitor Site Scraping	Gaining insights from the competitor site	AI can scrape competitor sites, collect data and send it to destinations needed	Browse AI, Scrap.so
Product Development	Product Creation Stage	Development of a product or service based on market research and customer personas and their need-gap	AI can analyze customer feedback and preferences to guide product development	Zeda, Qualtrics
Product Testing	Product Validation Stage	Testing of a product or service with a select group of customers	AI can analyze customer feedback during product testing to identify potential improvements	Conjointly, Testing AI

Live Case Study
AI-Powered Market Research and Product Development

Figure 11 - Launch of Fusion Cuisine Restaurant in Bali leveraging AI
(Source: Midjourney)

Context: Meet Marc, an innovative restaurateur preparing to launch "The Melting Pot," a unique fusion cuisine restaurant in Seminyak, Bali. Let's follow Marc's journey as he leverages AI for market research and product development.

✂ AI tools used:

- ChatGPT (For research, analysis, product development, and content creation)
- Looka (For logo and brand kit design)
- Scraphero (For scraping competitor reviews)
- Harpa AI (For generating Midjourney prompts)
- Midjourney (For restaurants and menu creatives)
- Bubble (No code app for digital menu)

💡 Step-by-Step Playbook

Step 1: Market Analysis and Opportunity Identification

Marc began his journey with **ChatGPT**, a powerful AI tool that provides a comprehensive market overview. It analyzed data on tourism recovery, demographics, consumption trends, and the competitive landscape in Seminyak, Bali. This high-level view helped Marc identify potential business opportunities and understand the challenges he might face. He identified "Summer Queen, Bali" as a key competitor and decided to delve deeper into their operations.

⚠ **Quick Note:** As mentioned earlier, every time you see the icon 💡, check out the live outputs and examples in the online reference provided to gain a practical perspective. You can bookmark these for easy reference.

Step 2: Business Plan Preparation

With a clear understanding of the market, Marc used **ChatGPT** to prepare a detailed business plan. The AI tool provided him with insights into the size of the market, the potential for his business, supportive factors, key watchouts, and the cost of operation. It also helped him draft a business model and a P&L proposal, which he could use to assess whether to bootstrap his business or seek investment. ChatGPT also aided Marc in identifying his competitive set and conducting a SWOT analysis, providing him with deeper insights into his competition.

Profit & Loss Items	Year 1 (USD)	Year 2 (USD)	Year 3 (USD)
Revenue	660,000	726,000	798,600
Cost of Goods Sold	-198,000	-217,800	-239,580
Gross Profit	462,000	508,200	559,020
Rent	-60,000	-63,000	-66,150
Salaries	-200,000	-210,000	-220,500
Utilities	-12,000	-12,600	-13,230
Marketing	-30,000	-31,500	-33,075
Miscellaneous	-20,000	-21,000	-22,050
Total Operating Expenses	-322,000	-338,100	-355,005
Net Profit Before Tax	140,000	170,100	204,015
Taxes (25%)	-35,000	-42,525	-51,004
Net Profit After Tax	105,000	127,575	153,011

Figure 12 - P&L Outlook for the Restaurant generated by ChatGPT

Step 3: Deep Dive into Customer Reviews

To understand his potential customers better, Marc used **ScrapeHero** to extract recent customer reviews of "Summer Queen, Bali." These reviews provided valuable insights into what customers like and dislike about the existing offerings. Marc fed these reviews into ChatGPT for sentiment analysis. This helped him understand customer preferences and identify gaps in the current offerings, which he could fill with his fusion cuisine restaurant.

	High Impact	Low Impact
Easy to Implement	**Service Improvement** • Conduct bi-weekly staff training on hospitality. • Ensure all staff have thorough product knowledge for menu recommendations.	**Ambiance** • Introduce dimmable lighting for cozy evening ambiance. • Establish rigorous cleanliness protocols, especially for high-traffic areas.
Hard to Implement	**Taste Preferences** • Continuously refine and test dishes with negative feedback, like Crispy Calamari. • Ensure premium dishes, like Wagyu Beef Tataki, maintain consistent quality in flavor and texture.	**Pricing** • Develop a range of affordable lunch specials, with dishes like fusion rice bowls. • Introduce dinner entrees with unique fusion flavors, priced between $18-$25.

Figure 13 - High-Level Recommendations by ChatGPT basis Scraping of Competitor Reviews

Step 4: Menu and Product Development

Marc leveraged AI to create a unique fusion menu catering to his target customers' tastes. He combined local ingredients with international flavors inspired by customer feedback. He used **Midjourney** to design a contemporary, warm, and culturally inspired restaurant ambiance. This ambiance, combined with a unique menu, provided a unique dining experience for his customers.

Step 5: Pricing Strategy

Marc researched the pricing of similar fusion cuisine restaurants in Seminyak, Bali. He used this information to determine a pricing strategy that aligned with customer expectations, ingredient costs, and profit margins. This strategy ensured that his restaurant is competitively priced while still profitable.

Category	Dish Name	Description	Price
Appetizers	Fusion Explosion	A creative dish combining flavors from different cuisines, such as Asian spices with a Western twist.	$22
Seafood	Crispy Calamari	Lightly fried calamari rings served with a tangy dipping sauce.	$12
	Seafood Symphony	A seafood platter featuring fresh catch of the day, including grilled prawns, seared scallops, and a tangy citrus glaze.	$28
	Spicy Tuna Poke Bowl	Marinated tuna, fresh vegetables, and Asian-inspired dressings atop a bed of rice or mixed greens.	$16
	Seared Sesame Salmon	Perfectly seared salmon fillet served with a ginger-infused sauce and a side of stir-fried vegetables.	$24
Vegetarian/Vegan	Miso Eggplant Stack	Layers of grilled eggplant, tofu, and miso glaze, topped with fresh herbs and sesame seeds.	$18
	Vegan Pad Thai	Plant-based version of the classic Thai dish, featuring rice noodles, tofu, and a medley of vegetables.	$15
Drinks	Sakura Martini	Premium gin, cherry blossom syrup, and a hint of citrus combine to create a floral-infused cocktail.	$12
	Mango Tango Mocktail	Refreshing blend of fresh mango, lime, and sparkling water.	$6

Figure 14 - Draft Menu Created by ChatGPT

Step 6: Digital Menu to Elevate the Ordering Experience

Marc used **Bubble** no code app developer platform to create a digital menu where people could look at dish details, customer reviews, and recommendations and then order directly. This gamification helped enrich the customer experience and brought a novelty factor to the restaurant.

Step 7: Customer Surveys and Feedback

Marc surveyed his target audience to gather feedback on their dining preferences and price sensitivity. He used AI survey analysis tools to create, process, and extract insights from the survey data. These insights helped him refine his menu and pricing strategy, ensuring they met his customers' needs and expectations.

Step 8: Product Testing and Refinement

Marc conducted taste tests and gathered feedback from a diverse group of individuals representing his target audience. He analyzed the feedback to refine and optimize his fusion dishes, ensuring they met the expectations and preferences of his customers. This iterative process of testing and refinement ensured that his restaurant's offerings were fine-tuned before the official launch.

Step 9: Iterative Improvements

After the launch of his fusion cuisine restaurant, Marc did not stop improving. He continuously monitored customer feedback, reviews, and ratings. He used AI tools to analyze the data and identify areas for improvement, such as menu adjustments, service enhancements, or introducing new dishes. This commitment to continuous improvement ensured that his restaurant stayed relevant and continued to meet the evolving needs of his customers.

In Conclusion

AI's transformative potential in market research and product development is undeniable. By harnessing AI's power, entrepreneurs like Marc can deepen their understanding of consumer behavior, predict market trends, and innovate products that resonate with consumers.

As we wrap up this chapter, remember that AI's power rests in its practical application. Are you now ready to discover how AI can elevate your branding and marketing efforts by 10x? Let us move to the next chapter—your gateway to AI-powered branding and marketing success!

BRANDING AND MARKETING: SUPERCHARGED BY AI

> *"Your brand is what other people say about you when you're not in the room."*
> *– Jeff Bezos*

*L*et me take you back in time when I was enduring one of my most intense stints. We were about to launch a product we believed would significantly impact our consumers' lives in Sri Lanka— mosquito repellant paper. Armed with exhaustive market research and product development findings, we had reached the battleground, the phase of branding and marketing.

The mission was clear; our responsibility was to create a powerful brand that would resonate with our target audience and craft a marketing strategy to propel our product into the limelight. We were a lean, agile team ready to take on the challenge, but the task before us was colossal.

Our first mission was to design the brand guidelines. We had to encapsulate our product's essence into a visual language that would form our brand's backbone. Then came the question of packaging—what kind of package would our product use? What shape, color, and design? What would be most effective in catching a customer's eye? And let's not forget the point-of-sale material. What should we use? What would create the maximum impact?

Planning the product's placement was a different ball game. Which stores should we choose? What planogram placement would yield the best results? We aimed to ensure our product was not just another item on the shelf but something that commanded attention.

Next, we delved into the storyboarding of our communications. What would be our narrative? How would we portray our product to the customers? This, of course, led to the design of advertisements and a partnership with a creative agency. The back and forth of creating and refining our marketing material was an exercise of patience and precision.

We then found ourselves in the labyrinth of media planning. Identifying the proper channels and the correct placements across these channels while balancing our budget was a complex dance. Determining the optimal price point from market and consumer perspectives was a tightrope walk.

As if we needed more than these challenges, we had to venture into the world of social media campaigns. How could we make our product stand out amidst the cacophony? Then came the task of identifying the right influencers to endorse our brand and ensure our message reaches the right audience.

And this was followed by PR, which included drafting PR briefs with the agency, fine-tuning them, and ensuring our story was conveyed effectively. It was all leading up to the grand finale—the launch event. Every detail, from start to end, needed meticulous planning.

All these operations, carried out for one product, took months of arduous work. The product was eventually launched, and the reception was gratifying. But as a leader, I couldn't help but question: how could we replicate this effort across our more extensive business portfolio with our lean and agile team? Could we have done this 10x faster?

This is where AI enters the picture. Every step of this journey, whether in marketing or branding, could be expedited and enhanced with AI. The challenges we faced, the time it consumed, and the hurdles we overcame all could be streamlined with AI.

As we move forward in this chapter, we'll dive deeper into AI's role in branding and marketing. We'll explore how it could revolutionize how we approach these crucial aspects of business, making the journey from conception to launch smoother, faster, and more efficient. And I can't help but think, if only we had harnessed the power of AI back then, how different things might have been!

The Conventional Way of Branding and Marketing

The inception of any successful business venture begins with branding and marketing. Branding is creating a distinctive identity for your product or service. This includes defining your brand's mission, values, personality, positioning, and visual elements, such as logos and color schemes.

On the other hand, marketing refers to the act of promoting your brand. to potential customers. It includes market research, customer segmentation, product development, pricing, distribution, advertising, and public relations.

These processes, while crucial, are time-consuming, labor-intensive, and require expertise in various areas. The increasing complexity of the consumer market, combined with the information overload experienced by consumers, further complicates the branding and marketing processes.

Moreover, conventional methods often rely on intuition, assumptions, and static customer data, which may lead to inaccurate targeting, unappealing messaging, and ineffective marketing campaigns. More precise, efficient, and effective branding and marketing methods are needed.

Enter Artificial Intelligence

Artificial Intelligence (AI) offers an innovative solution to these challenges. AI can scan vast volumes of data and find patterns that humans cannot see. It can analyze customer behavior, predict future trends, and automate routine tasks.

As we look ahead, the future of branding and marketing with AI seems promising. Technology is evolving rapidly, and businesses are finding innovative ways to harness its power. Here are a few trends to watch out for:

Hyper-Personalization: We expect to see even more personalized experiences as AI evolves. Brands can tailor their messaging and offerings to individual customers based on their behavior, preferences, and even mood. This level of personalization will enhance customer engagement and increase brand loyalty.

Real-Time Marketing: With AI, brands will be able to respond to market changes and customer behavior in real-time. This could involve adjusting marketing campaigns on the fly, responding to customer queries instantly, or even predicting and preempting customer needs.

Voice and Visual Search: As more consumers use voice assistants and visual search, brands must adapt their marketing strategies accordingly. AI will be quintessential in optimizing voice and visual search content, ensuring that brands remain visible and relevant.

AI-Generated Content: AI is already being used to generate straightforward content like news articles and social media posts. As the technology improves, we can expect AI to create more complex content, such as ad copy, blog posts, and even video content.

Predictive Analytics: AI will continue to enhance its predictive capabilities, providing brands with more accurate forecasts of market trends, customer behavior, and campaign performance.

This will enable brands to make more informed decisions and stay ahead of the competition.

In conclusion, AI can potentially revolutionize how we approach branding and marketing. It can provide deeper insights, streamline operations, and enable personalization at scale. However, it's important to remember that AI is a tool to complement humans, not replace human creativity and strategic thinking. The most successful brands will be those that combine AI's power with a deep understanding of their customers and a compelling brand story.

As we step into this exciting future, I can't help but reflect on my mosquito repellant paper launch journey. If we had the power of AI back then, how different things might have been! But as they say, hindsight is 20/20. The important thing is to learn from our experiences and embrace the opportunities that lie ahead. And with AI in our toolkit, the future of branding and marketing looks brighter than ever. But how does this all work in practice? Look at real-world examples of brands successfully incorporating AI into their branding and marketing efforts.

Real-Life Examples

Virgin Voyages: Sailing into the Future with AI

Imagine receiving a personalized invitation to sail the high seas from none other than Jennifer Lopez herself. Sounds like a dream, right? But for Virgin Voyages, it's a reality crafted with the power of AI.

In a recent campaign, Virgin Voyages introduced 'Jen AI', an AI-powered virtual version of Jennifer Lopez. This AI avatar of

J-Lo invites people to experience the luxury of a Virgin Voyage. But the magic doesn't stop there. As part of the campaign, consumers can create their own custom invitations using the Jen AI tool on VirginVoyages.com.

The campaign, created with advertising agency VMLY&R and AI agency Deeplocal, is a playful and innovative use of generative AI. The result is a personalized, engaging, and memorable brand experience that stands out in the crowded travel market.

The 'Jen AI' campaign is a testament to the transformative power of AI in branding and marketing. It showcases how AI can create personalized and engaging content, generate buzz, and provide a unique brand experience. It's not just about using AI for the sake of technology but about integrating AI to enhance the brand's identity, engage the audience, and ultimately drive business results.

This innovative campaign is a prime example of how AI can revolutionize branding and marketing. It demonstrates the potential of AI to create personalized, engaging, and memorable brand experiences, setting a new standard for the industry. As we move forward, integrating AI into branding and marketing strategies is not just an exciting possibility; it's an essential step for brands looking to stay competitive in the digital age.

Coca-Cola: Crafting Art with AI Magic

Dive into a real-world application of AI, where the effervescence of innovation meets the timeless allure of an iconic brand—Coca-Cola.

Imagine standing in a bustling city square. The familiar red and white logo of Coca-Cola shines brightly, but this time, it's not just an invitation to savor a refreshing drink. It's a call to craft art with AI, to blend your creativity with the brand's iconic imagery.

This is the magic of Coca-Cola's "Create Real Magic" platform. Developed in collaboration with OpenAI and Bain & Company, it's a space where digital creators worldwide can harness the power of GPT-4 and DALL-E to generate original artwork using assets from Coca-Cola's rich archives. From the classic contour bottle to the beloved Coca-Cola Santa Claus, artists are given a unique canvas for AI-powered experimentation.

But this isn't just about art. It's about co-creation, about blending the brand's storied history with the boundless potential of AI. In its pioneering spirit, Coca-Cola has opened its brand to global digital creatives, democratizing its iconic imagery and ushering in a new era of collaboration.

And the results? They're not just digital doodles but masterpieces sculpted by the combined might of cutting-edge AI and human imagination. It's a testament to Coca-Cola's commitment to innovation and exploring the intersections of tradition and technology.

So, the next time you're drawn to that iconic Coca-Cola logo, remember it's more than a drink. It's a fusion of history and innovation, a dance of flavors and algorithms, and a testament to the transformative power of AI in reshaping our everyday experiences.

Cadbury: Elevated Brand Engagement with AI-Powered Personalization

Among the array of brands that leveraged AI for creative marketing, Cadbury's Diwali campaign in India, dubbed 'NotJustACadburyAd,' stood out as a brilliant testament to the fusion of technology, culture, and social consciousness. Recognizing the financial strain faced by local businesses due to the Covid-19 pandemic, Cadbury turned to AI, offering these businesses a unique opportunity. Through a special campaign, local store owners were given the chance to design their own commercials with Bollywood megastar Shah Rukh Khan endorsing their shops. By simply logging onto a dedicated website and sharing details about their store, proprietors harnessed AI and machine learning tools to produce a tailor-made ad with Khan's likeness speaking their brand's name.

Integrating AI Across the Branding and Marketing Funnel

The application of AI can span the entire branding and marketing funnel. Here's a step-by-step guide on how to integrate AI at each stage to create a robust strategy:

- **Brand Toolkit**: Tools like Looka can be used to develop a cohesive brand identity. Using artificial intelligence, Looka considers your preferences to generate several logo options, helps select color palettes and typography and ensures that your brand's visual identity aligns with your brand values and resonates with your target audience. Another interesting AI tool, Namelix, uses AI algorithms to generate unique and catchy brand names and logos based on your business specifics, at the click of a button.

- **Packaging Design**: Designing packaging that aligns with your brand image and appeals to customers can be daunting. AI platforms like Midjourney can assist in this process by providing creative visualization. You can get various design options for packages, which you can test virtually for consumer appeal and practicality. This can also significantly shorten the iterations with the design and packaging team, increasing the go-to-market speed for any new product.
- **Merchandising:** AI tools such as Spring Global can also help in creating engaging merch. By analyzing customer behavior and preferences, these tools can provide recommendations for promotional signage, display materials, and optimal shelf positioning that are likely to attract and engage customers in physical retail locations.
- **Storyboarding and Advertising**: AI can streamline the advertising process. Platforms like Celtra use AI to automate the design process, ensuring brand consistency across all ad sizes and formats. By generating multiple ad variations, testing them, and optimizing them based on performance, you can enhance the effectiveness of your advertisements.
- **Media Planning**: AI can play a significant role in optimizing media buying decisions. Albert, for instance, leverages AI to optimize ad spending, experimenting with different media mix models and suggesting where to invest for the best return on investment. This allows you to maximize your reach and impact while staying within your budget.
- **Planograms and Store Placement**: Optimizing product placement in retail stores can significantly enhance visibility

and sales. AI tools like Nexgen POG can analyze sales data, customer behavior, and other factors to generate optimal planograms and store layouts, maximizing product visibility and enhancing the customer shopping experience.

- **Social Media:** AI tools like Buffer, Emplifi or Hootsuite can significantly enhance your social media strategy. They can analyze past post performance and user engagement to suggest the optimal time to post content. They also offer features like post-scheduling and performance tracking, freeing up time for you to focus on content creation.
- **Online Shopping:** AI can personalize the online shopping experience. By analyzing user behavior and preferences, AI can recommend products, offer personalized discounts, and suggest add-on items for customers. Tools like Clerk.io use machine learning to continually learn from customer interactions and improve their recommendations over time.
- **PR:** In the realm of PR, AI tools like Signal AI can help you keep a pulse on how your brand is perceived in the media. By analyzing news articles, blog posts, social media posts, and other forms of media, these tools can provide insights into the sentiment about your brand and better understand how your PR efforts are performing.
- **Launch Event:** AI tools like Bizzabo can help streamline the process when planning a

launch event. They can analyze past event data to suggest the best format, identify potential speakers, and recommend promotional strategies. These tools can also automate many logistical aspects of event planning, allowing you to focus on delivering a memorable experience for attendees.

These steps show the power of AI in creating a comprehensive and successful branding and marketing strategy. AI can significantly boost your efforts by providing deeper insights, automating repetitive tasks, and allowing for scale personalization. It's about combining the best of what AI offers with human creativity and strategic thinking. That's where the real magic happens.

AI-Powered Marketing

Stage Name	Stage Description	What Happens	How AI Can Help	Example AI Tools
Attraction	Awareness Stage	Potential customers become aware of your product or service	AI can drive awareness through SEO optimization and targeted advertising	Surfer SEO, Google Ads, Smartly.io
Engagement	Interest Stage	Potential customers are interested and interact with your brand	AI can create personalized experiences and engage users with AI-driven chatbots, content curation, and product recommendations	Botpress, HubSpot, Tidio

	Decision Stage	Engaged customers decide to purchase	AI utilizes predictive analytics and personalized recommendation systems to convert leads into sales	Klaviyo, Salesforce
Conversion				
Retention	Action Stage	Building relationships with the customers post-purchase for repeat business	AI helps in analyzing customer behavior, predicting churn, and developing personalized follow-ups	Zoho CRM, Optimove
Advocacy	Loyalty Stage	Turn customers into brand advocates	AI can analyze customer satisfaction, predict potential advocates, and use NLP to analyze customer feedback	Yotpo, AskNicely, Antavo

Live Case Study
AI Integration Across Branding and Marketing

Figure 15 - Launching D2C Luxury Ayurveda Skincare Brand, Divyaveda, Using AI (Source: Midjourney)

Context: In this case study, we follow the journey of Amit, a solopreneur launching a new D2C brand, "Divyaveda," a luxury Ayurveda skincare line. Leveraging AI tools, Amit streamlines and boosts each step of his branding and marketing process for the product launch.

⚒ AI tools used:

- ChatGPT, with additional plugins (For brand content, image prompts, etc.)
- Looka (For brand logo and toolkit)
- Midjourney & Canva (For packaging and point-of-sale material design)
- Framer AI (For website creation)
- Bubble (No code app)
- Zapier (For email marketing automation)
- Eleven Labs (For text-to-speech creation and voice cloning)
- D-ID (For video generation)
- Jasper AI (For copywriting)

💡 Step-by-Step Playbook

Step 1: Market Research and Customer Insights

Amit started his journey by leveraging **ChatGPT** to conduct comprehensive market research. The AI tool provided him with a high-level view of the luxury Ayurveda skincare market, including key competitors, market size, and growth trends. It also helped him identify the target customer persona, lifestyle, preferences, and pain points. This detailed understanding of the market and customer insights formed the foundation for Amit's branding and marketing strategy.

> **Brand Brief: Luxury Ayurveda Skincare Brand**
>
> **Target Customer Persona**
>
> Name: Aanya Kapoor Age: 30-45 Gender: Female Occupation: High-income professional Lifestyle: Active, health-conscious, prefers natural and organic products Interests: Yoga, meditation, holistic wellness Values: Authenticity, self-care, sustainability *Pain Points:* Concerns about aging, stress, skin health, pollution, and desire for a luxurious skincare experience *Desired Benefits:* Effective skincare solutions, natural and high-quality ingredients, holistic wellness experience, luxury packaging, and branding
>
> **Brand Elements**
>
> a. Brand Identity:
> - **Aesthetic:** Modern, sophisticated, and luxurious
> - **Colors:** Earthy tones, incorporating rich, jewel-like colors to evoke a sense of luxury and nature
> - **Typography:** Elegant and refined fonts that convey a balance of tradition and modernity
> - **Logo:** A minimalistic yet distinctive logo that represents the brand's connection to Ayurveda and luxury
>
> b. Packaging:
> - Premium materials: Use high-quality packaging materials like glass, sustainable plastics, and eco-friendly options
> - Design: Elegant and minimalistic Packaging with intricate detailing, reflecting the brand's Ayurvedic heritage and luxury positioning
> - Labels: Clear and informative labels that highlight the product's natural and organic ingredients, along with the benefits they offer
>
> c. Communication:
> - Tone: A balance of scientific expertise and a holistic approach, promoting the idea of a complete skincare experience
> - Messaging: Emphasize the brand's commitment to using authentic Ayurvedic ingredients, luxury, and efficacy
> - Imagery: Use high-resolution images featuring natural elements, serene settings, and diverse models to showcase the brand's inclusivity and effectiveness
>
> **Brand Name**
>
> "Divyaveda" Explanation: "Divya" means divine in Sanskrit, while "Veda" represents the ancient Indian scriptures associated with Ayurveda. The name Divyaveda conveys a sense of luxury, authenticity, and the divine nature of Ayurvedic skincare.
>
> **Slogan**
>
> "Unlock Your Skin's Natural Radiance" Explanation: This slogan captures the essence of the brand, emphasizing the transformative and illuminating effects of the skincare products. It resonates with the target customer persona's desire for a luxurious Ayurveda experience that enhances their natural beauty.
>
> *Divyaveda encapsulates the spirit of luxury and Ayurveda, offering premium skincare products that help customers discover their inner radiance.*

Figure 16 - Brand Brief Created by ChatGPT

Step 2: Brand Identity and Positioning

With a clear understanding of the market and his target customers, Amit used **Looka**, an AI-powered design tool, to create a unique logo and brand kit for Divyaveda. The tool generated several design options based on Amit's inputs about the brand's personality and values. He selected a logo and brand kit that best embodied the essence of luxury, nature, and wellness, aligning with Divyaveda's positioning as a luxury Ayurvedic skincare line.

Figure 17 - AI-Generated Divyaveda Brand Logo (Source: Midjourney)

Step 3: Packaging Design

Next, Amit uses **Midjourney**, an AI-driven design tool, to create unique packaging designs for Divyaveda's products. The AI tool generated multiple design options based on Amit's preferences, allowing him to visualize different packaging options and choose the one that best aligns with Divyaveda's brand identity. This process ensured that the packaging is functional, visually appealing, and resonated with the target customers.

Figure 18 - Draft Packaging Design Created with Midjourney

Step 4: Point of Sales Material and Merchandising

For point-of-sales materials and merchandising, Amit uses **Midjourney** and **Canva**. These AI tools helped him create visually appealing display materials, promotional signage, and other visual elements that strengthen Divyaveda's brand image and appeal to his target customers. The tools also allowed him to experiment with different designs and formats, ensuring that the materials effectively attracted and engaged customers.

Step 5: Developing Marketing Content

Amit used **ChatGPT** and **Jasper AI** to create engaging marketing content. These AI tools helped him draft SEO-friendly blog content, landing pages, and product descriptions. The AI tools also suggested keywords and phrases that can enhance Divyaveda's online presence and visibility. This ensured that the content is both engaging and optimized for search engines, increasing the chances of reaching a wider audience.

Step 6: Website Creation

Amit uses **Framer AI** to create a visually appealing and user-friendly website for Divyaveda. The AI tool allowed him to create a fully functional website quickly and efficiently, providing a seamless online brand experience for his customers. The tool also provided suggestions for website layout and design based on the latest trends and best practices, ensuring the website was modern and engaging.

https://divyaveda.framer.ai/

Step 7: Personalized Marketing Funnel

Amit integrated customer signup forms with **ChatGPT**, creating a personalized marketing funnel. ChatGPT, equipped with the brand content repository, product usage instructions, etc., generated customized responses for each customer based on their need and specifics like age or skin type, which were then funneled into an email marketing drip campaign via Zapier. This ensured that each customer receives personalized communication and product recommendations suited to their need, enhancing their engagement with the brand and increasing the chances of conversion.

Step 8: Social Media Marketing

Amit used **ChatGPT, Midjourney, Canva, ElevenLabs**, and **D-ID** together to create engaging written, visual, audio and video content for Divyaveda's social media channels. These AI tools helped him create a social media plan, design visually appealing posts, and generate viral video content. The tools also provided insights into the best times to post and the type of content that resonates with his audience, helping him build a strong base of followers in a short time.

*Refer to the exercise we did in the chapter on prompt engineering for creating the social media plan for Divyaveda.

Step 9: Building Expertise in Skin Care with a Custome Skin Expert App

Amit used **Bubble** to create a simple and functional no-code app that customers can use to enter their personal details and skin types to get custom products and lifestyle recommendations for healthy skin. This helped Amit engage and retain the customers and also significantly increases the brand's lifetime value.

Step 10: Monitoring and Optimization

Finally, Amit used Google Analytics and **Brandwatch** to monitor Divyaveda's performance and identify opportunities for improvement. These tools provided insights into site performance, customer feedback, and customer trends, helping Amit refine his products and marketing strategy. They also alerted him to any potential issues or opportunities in real time, allowing him to make quick adjustments and maintain a high level of customer satisfaction.

In conclusion, Amit's journey illustrates how AI can turbocharge the branding and marketing process, from market research to social media marketing. Solopreneurs like Amit can streamline their operations, enhance their marketing efforts, and drive better business outcomes by leveraging AI tools.

Whether you're a solopreneur or part of a larger team, AI can help you 10x your branding and marketing efforts. Stay tuned for the next chapter, where we delve into how AI revolutionizes sales and business development by 10x.

AMPLIFY YOUR SALES AND BUSINESS DEVELOPMENT WITH AI

> *"Don't find customers for your products; find products for your customers."*
> *– Seth Godin*

*R*ewind the clock with me for a moment to a few years back when I was navigating the complexities of leading B2B sales and business development for a fast-paced, dynamic company. It felt akin to performing a delicate juggling act, with countless balls in the air and the audience eagerly waiting for your next move.

Our journey began with lead generation, identifying potential partners who could augment our platform's value. Through countless Google searches, competitor site scraping, and market exploration, we amassed a list of thousands of leads. But that was just the start. The daunting task ahead was qualifying these leads, identifying the ones aligned with our platform's vision, and dismissing the rest.

Having identified our potential partners, we began the painstaking process of personalized outreach. Crafting unique, compelling messages that would resonate with each potential partner was a task that demanded attention to detail and consumed enormous amounts of time.

Then came the pitch. To convince prospective partners to board our platform, we had to present our offering persuasively, tailoring our proposition to align with their needs and expectations.

But securing their agreement was just the end of the first leg of our journey. The subsequent multi-step onboarding process could span several days, with each step meticulously designed to ensure our new partner was optimally set up for success on our platform. And that was just the business development aspect of the role. With the platform set and the partners on board, the sales process was about to begin.

Account managing tens of thousands of partners was a Herculean task, requiring strategic planning and prioritization. We needed to identify the partners with the highest potential, segment them based on their relevance to our offerings, and approach them with the most suitable pitches. This process was like navigating a labyrinth to effectively cross-sell and upsell our offerings to drive revenue growth and achieve our core sales objectives.

We also had to identify new business opportunities for our partners, digging deep into heaps of data to uncover potential gold mines. And the challenge was equally daunting on our end. Analyzing voluminous data daily to discern business opportunities, unlock potential growth, and determine what needed prioritizing was a complex task. All these efforts aimed to upskill our team continuously, provide them with relevant data points, and prepare them to convert potential partners effectively.

Reflecting on this intricate process, I pondered: Could we have achieved this 10x faster? Was there a way to optimize our workflow, decipher data more intuitively, and bolster growth? And that's when AI entered the picture.

Embracing Salesforce and integrating AI revolutionized our workflow. AI helped us streamline processes, understand large data volumes better, and present our team with the right opportunities. It assisted us in prioritizing tasks, improving efficiency, and equipped us with relevant data points for more effective partner conversations. The result was faster partner conversion and accelerated business growth, enabling us to become a more efficient sales and business development organization.

This was a snapshot of my experience and how AI dramatically transformed our B2B sales and business development processes. The real story of AI's potential to power sales and business organizations to work 10x faster and more efficiently is far more profound, and we will explore it in this chapter.

The Conventional Way

Picture yourself as an entrepreneur today, running your business in the current conventional way without the power of AI. Your day is filled to the brim with many tasks that, though necessary, seem to drain away your hours, leaving you with little time to focus on strategic growth.

You're wading through a sea of potential leads in sales, determining which ones are most likely to convert. You're making countless calls, sending numerous emails, analyzing data, negotiating deals, and even attending networking events to connect with potential clients. You're spending precious time manually entering data, following up on leads, and maintaining client relationships. It's all essential, but there's no denying it's a lot of work.

While these efforts are the backbone of your business, they present a range of challenges. The first hurdle is time. With only so many hours in the day, your team's time could be better spent on more strategic, revenue-generating tasks. Secondly, manual data collection and analysis methods leave room for human error, potentially leading to misinformed decisions. Lastly, with access to data-driven insights, predicting market trends or understanding customer behavior can be more accessible.

In a nutshell, the conventional approach, while functional, comes with its limitations. It's time-consuming and prone to human error. It needs predictive abilities, all of which can curb your business's potential for growth. The following section will discover how AI can address these challenges, offering a transformative solution to supercharge your sales and business development efforts. Let's turn the page and enter the world of AI.

Enter Artificial Intelligence

Imagine a different reality where AI takes up your routine tasks, automates them, and performs them more efficiently. This new reality is not a futuristic dream; it's the world today, transformed by the power of Artificial Intelligence.

In the realm of sales, AI is a game changer. You no longer have to sift through countless leads manually. Instead, an AI-powered tool can scan hundreds of profiles in minutes, scoring and ranking them based on their conversion likelihood. It's like having a tireless assistant who never takes a break and keeps your sales pipeline updated.

The benefits of AI continue. Let's consider personalizing your sales approach. With traditional methods, crafting a personalized pitch for each prospect can be time-consuming. With AI, however, you can automate this process. AI can analyze a prospect's digital footprints, understanding their needs, preferences, and habits. It can then craft a personalized pitch that speaks directly to the prospect's unique requirements. This results in more impactful conversations and increased conversion rates. In addition, AI can also help analyze customer behavior and preferences and help cross-sell and up-sell relevant products, leading to an increased share of wallets with customers.

In business development, AI opens a whole new world of opportunities. Analyzing market trends, which once required hours of manual work, can now be done instantly with AI-powered predictive analytics tools. These tools can analyze vast volumes of data and provide accurate forecasts about market trends, helping you make informed decisions and stay ahead of the curve.

AI acts as a force multiplier for your sales and business development efforts. It automates repetitive tasks, delivers data-driven insights, enables personalization at scale, provides predictive abilities, and so much more. With AI, you can operate at a higher level of efficiency and accuracy, ensuring your business is primed for growth. But how does this AI transformation look in the real world? Let us dive into some real-life examples in the next section.

Real-Life Example:
Salesforce: The AI-Driven Sales Powerhouse

When you interact with Salesforce's platform, you engage with more than just a CRM system. You're tapping into a potent AI engine revolutionizing how Salesforce operates and serves its customers.

Salesforce's commitment to AI is epitomized by Einstein, an integrated AI layer that enhances the platform's capabilities. Einstein is designed to analyze vast amounts of data, automate tasks, and provide insights, all aimed at boosting productivity and enriching customer experiences.

One of the standout features of Einstein is its predictive analytics. Within the Sales Cloud and Service Cloud, Einstein can forecast sales opportunities, recommend next-best actions, and even automate routine tasks, thereby enhancing the productivity of sales representatives and service agents.

But Einstein's capabilities don't stop at sales and service. Across Salesforce's suite of products, Einstein provides insights, automates processes, and personalizes user experiences, whether it's in marketing, e-commerce, or analytics.

So, as you delve deeper into Salesforce's ecosystem, remember that it's not just a CRM tool. It's a sophisticated platform that harnesses the power of AI to redefine customer engagement, sales processes, and business analytics.

However, the advantages of AI aren't exclusive to tech giants. Whether you're a large enterprise or a solopreneur, you can integrate AI into your sales and business development strategies. The subsequent sections will guide you on weaving AI throughout the sales cycle.

Integrating AI Across the Sales Cycle

The application of AI can span the entire sales cycle, from lead generation to customer retention. Here's a step-by-step guide on how to integrate AI at each stage to create a robust sales strategy:

- **Lead Generation:** AI tools like Growbots and LeadFuze can automate finding new leads. These tools use AI to scour the internet, identify potential leads based on your criteria, and even initiate contact with them. This can save you countless hours of manual searching and outreach.
- **Lead Scoring:** Once you have a list of potential leads, AI can help you prioritize them. Tools like Freshsales analyze various data points about each lead and score them based on their likelihood to convert, allowing you to focus your efforts on the most promising leads.
- **Personalized Outreach:** AI can also help you personalize your outreach to each lead. Tools like Exceed.ai can analyze a lead's digital footprints to understand their needs and preferences. They can then craft personalized messages that resonate with each lead, increasing the chances of a positive response. Also,

tools like Sendspark can help you send personalized videos at scale, increasing the chances of conversion.

- **Sales Forecasting:** AI can provide more accurate sales forecasts, helping you make informed business decisions. Tools like Akkio use AI to analyze historical sales data and predict future sales trends, helping you plan your sales strategy more effectively.
- **Cross-Selling and Upselling:** AI can also help you identify opportunities for cross-selling and upselling. Tools like Obviously use AI to analyze a customer's purchase history and suggest related products they might be interested in, which can help you increase your average transaction value and boost your revenue.
- **Customer Retention:** Finally, AI can help you retain your existing customers. Tools like ChurnZero use AI to analyze customer behavior and predict which customers are at risk of churning. This allows you to proactively address their concerns and improve their experience, increasing their likelihood of staying with your business.

Integrating AI across your sales cycle allows you to automate repetitive tasks, gain deeper insights into your customers, and make more informed business decisions. This can help you increase sales efficiency, improve customer relationships, and grow your business.

AI-Powered Sales and Business Development

Stage Name	Stage Description	What Happens	How AI Can Help	Example AI Tools
Lead Generation	Prospecting Stage	Identify potential customers who might be interested in your products or services	AI can help in smart prospecting by identifying high potential leads based on historical data and predictive analysis	LinkedIn Sales Navigator, Apollo.io
Lead Nurturing	Engagement Stage	Engaging with the identified leads through various channels to warm them up	AI can help in creating personalized content and automated follow-ups. It can predict the right time and channel to reach out	Marketo, Mailchimp, Tavus.io

Conversion	Decision Stage	Leads make the decision to purchase or use your product or service	AI can enhance sales forecasting and leverage predictive analytics to improve conversion rate	HubSpot, Salesforce, SalesDirector.ai, Exceed.ai
Customer Retention	Retention Stage	Retaining the customers post-purchase	AI can analyze customer behavior, create personalized offers, and predict churn to improve customer retention	Gainsight, Zoho, Primer AI
Sales Performance Analysis	Analysis	Analyzing the performance of the sales team and the effectiveness of sales strategies	AI can provide insights into sales performance and detect buying signals	People.ai, Tableau GPT

Live Case Study
AI-Powered Business Development and Sales

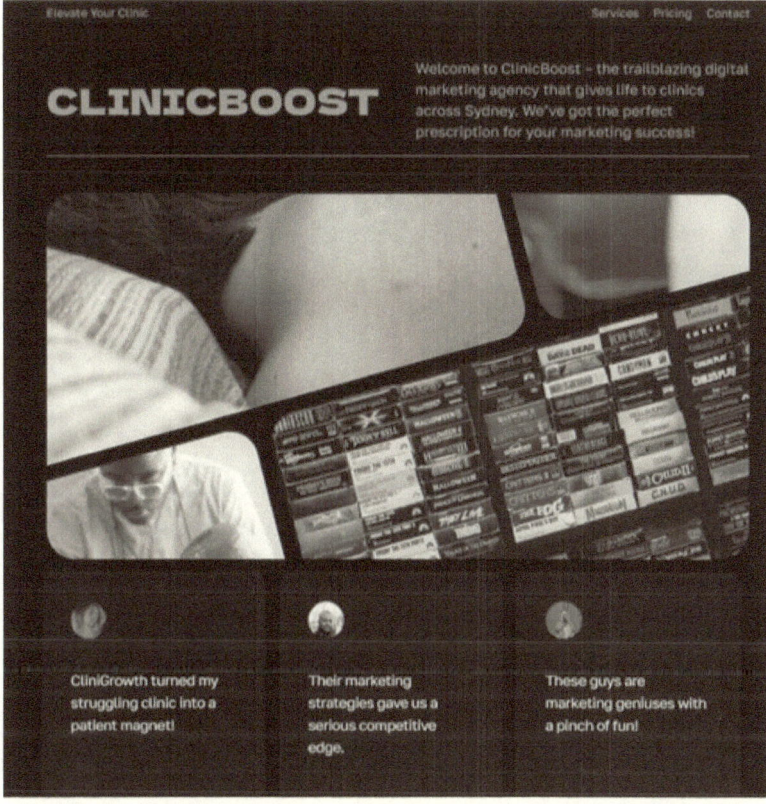

Figure 19 - ClinicBoost Website Generated by AI (Source: Midjourney)

Context: Meet Amelia, a dynamic and ambitious entrepreneur based in Sydney. She recently launched her startup, "ClinicBoost," a digital marketing agency that helps local clinics enhance their online presence. Let's explore Amelia's playbook, which leverages AI to amplify her business development and sales initiatives.

⚒ AI tools used:

- ChatGPT, with additional plugins (For content creation, custom emails, etc.)
- Apollo.io (For lead generation)
- Zapier (For automation)
- Sendspark (For sending personalized video at scale)
- Calendly (For auto appointment booking)
- Framer AI (For portfolio website creation)
- Crystal Knows (For understanding lead archetype)

💡 Step-by-Step Playbook

Here is the step-by-step workflow for your reference:

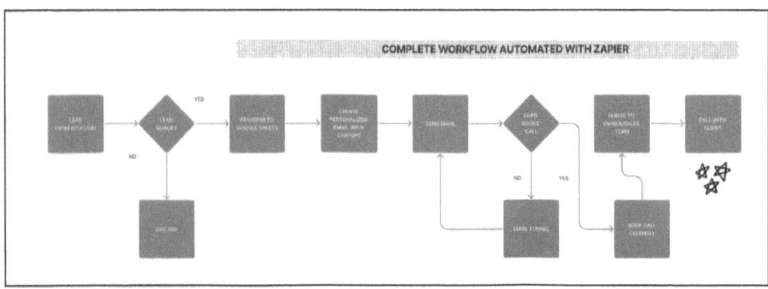

Figure 20 - Workflow for AI Integration Created with Figma Tool

Step 1: Building a Stellar Portfolio

Amelia started using **ChatGPT** to draft compelling content pieces, client testimonials, and case studies, demonstrating her digital marketing prowess. She used **Framer AI** to design a visually appealing and intuitive portfolio webpage highlighting her agency's capabilities.

Step 2: Prospecting Leads

She then employed **Apollo.io** and **LinkedIn's Sales Navigator** to compile a list of potential clients—clinics across Sydney that could benefit from her services. She tailored her search to identify clinics with minimal or lackluster online presence, presenting the perfect opportunity for her agency.

Figure 21 Sample of Curated Leads List from Apollo.io

Step 3: Streamlining Processes with Automation

Amelia integrated her lead generation tools with **Zapier**, automating several tasks. Zapier swiftly added the new leads to her CRM system, sent introductory emails, and assigned tasks to her sales team, ensuring a seamless and efficient workflow.

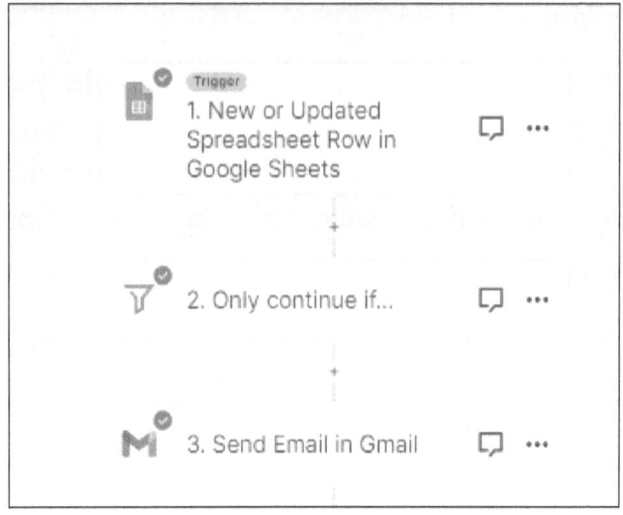

Figure 22 - Zapier Workflow Automation

Step 4: Crafting and Sending Personalized Cold Emails

To initiate contact, Amelia relied on **ChatGPT** to help construct engaging, personalized cold emails that cater to each clinic's unique needs and concerns. Then, she personalized the mail drafted with ChatGPT via Zapier and sent it across, which helped her maintain a high open and response rate, putting her one step closer to her prospects. Amelia used tools like **Crystal Knows,** which helped her understand the lead archetype to be more persuasive with both written and verbal communication. Amelia also used **ChatGPT** to create personalized lead magnets, like free E-books relevant to her target audience, to get her potential customers to subscribe to the mailing list even if they are not immediately ready for a conversation.

In addition, Amelia also used **Sendspark** to create and send out personalized videos at a 10x scale to high-value leads, which helps with a better conversion rate.

Step 5: Scheduling Appointments

Once a clinic shows interest, it's time to arrange a consultation. Amelia used **Calendly**, integrated with her email and calendar system, allowing leads to book an appointment that works for everyone effortlessly. This saves time and eliminates any scheduling confusion.

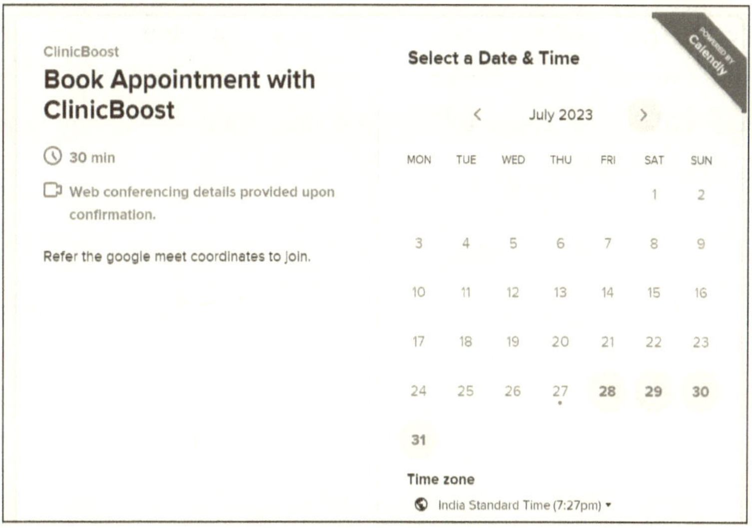

Figure 23 - Automated Calendly Invite for Appointment Scheduling

By strategically deploying AI across her business development and sales processes, Amelia ensured ClinicBoost operates optimally, saves valuable time, and improves conversion rates. This approach illustrates how meticulous planning and the intelligent use of AI can supercharge a startup's growth trajectory by 10x, regardless of size or budget.

However, it's important to remember that AI is a tool to support us and not a replacement for human creativity and strategic thinking. The most successful businesses will be those that combine AI's power with a deep understanding of their customers and a compelling sales strategy.

As we step into this exciting future, I can't help but reflect on my journey. If I had the power of AI back then in my sales and business development roles, how different things might have been! The important thing is to learn from our experiences and embrace the opportunities that lie ahead. And with AI in our toolkit, the future of sales and business development looks brighter than ever.

AI-DRIVEN STRATEGY, PLANNING, AND ANALYTICS

> *"However beautiful the strategy, you should occasionally look at the results."*
> *— Winston*

Let me share an episode from my tenure as an area sales leader for a prominent consumer organization in India. I was responsible for a mammoth task—setting up and scaling a sub-distributor network from scratch.

The complexity of the task was unprecedented. Decisions had to be made about which markets to penetrate, which retailers to collaborate with, and which products to stock in their outlets. We also had to decide on the volume of each product to be stocked at each retailer, ensuring a delicate balance to avoid returns or stock shortages. Furthermore, positioning the products on the shelves was crucial in driving maximum sales. Each decision had a downstream impact, making every choice critical for the overall sales and growth strategy.

Given our operations' complex, interconnected nature—with super stockists, sub-stockists, and retailers—collecting and analyzing data was pivotal. But this was a challenging task. It meant wrangling with numerous data points, wrestling with spreadsheets, and making sense of Tableau reports. The process was time-consuming and laden with trial and error, leading to delayed decisions and, sometimes, corrective actions.

And it wasn't just about us. We had to empower our extended stakeholders—the super stockists and sub-stockists—to access their data and business insights. This was essential for their ROI and, subsequently, for maintaining our relationships with them. I remember creating extensive Excel macros to assist these sub-stockists, a tedious task fraught with manual work and trial-and-error processes.

Reflecting on those times, I envisioned a toolkit to streamline these processes. One that would assist us in collecting and organizing data, analyzing it, and providing strategic insights. We needed a tool that would guide us in prioritizing markets, retailers, and products. We needed a tool that would alert us to opportunities and challenges, give us a competitive analysis, and help us strategize effectively. If we had access to such a tool, we could have built a more robust and agile strategy and executed it at rocket speed.

Fast forward to the present, and that vision is now a reality. With the advent of AI tools, the challenges I encountered as a business leader are now surmountable. AI can streamline the processes of data collection, organization, and analysis. It can provide strategic insights, highlight opportunities, flag potential issues, and guide decision-making.

This chapter will explore AI's transformative power in strategy, planning, and analytics. We will explore how AI tools can turbocharge your business planning and design, driving 10x growth and efficiency. Hold onto your seats as we embark on this exciting journey.

The Conventional Way

Picture this: You are preparing for the strategic plan of your business. You start by collecting massive amounts of information from various sources—sales records, market reports, customer feedback, and competitor analysis. The challenge begins with making sense of this data sprawl, each piece of information seeming crucial for decision-making.

So, you start organizing this data. Manual data entry into spreadsheets becomes your daily routine. Rows upon rows, columns upon columns, the data stacks up, forming a labyrinth that you need to navigate. You're not just dealing with numbers; you're dealing with different data formats from various sources, which add complexity to the task.

Then comes the analysis phase. You start looking for patterns, trends, and insights within the vast sea of numbers. You dive deep into the data, slicing and dicing it in countless ways to unearth actionable insights. It's like finding a needle in a haystack, and it keeps moving!

And then, there's the decision-making phase. After days of data manipulation, you sit down with your team to discuss the insights and plan your strategic moves. Your reliance is heavily on the data in front of you, your past experiences, and your gut instinct. You debate, brainstorm, and make decisions that will steer your business's future.

This conventional approach, while still being the backbone of strategic planning in many businesses, comes with numerous challenges:

Time and Resource Intensive: From data collection to decision-making, each step is manual, time-consuming, and labor-intensive. It's not uncommon to spend days or even weeks in this process.

Prone to Errors: Manual data handling is often associated with human errors. A minor data entry or analysis error can lead to significant missteps in strategic decisions.

Limited Capacity for Data Analysis: How much data you can handle manually is limited. This restricts your ability to deal with large volumes of data, limiting your insights' depth and breadth.

Reliance on Human Instinct: Despite all the data, the final decisions are often based on human intuition. While intuition has its place, over-reliance on it can lead to bias and prevent you from making the most effective decisions.

Slow Response: The conventional approach can delay decision-making, causing slower responses to market changes. In today's fast-paced business world, being slow to adapt can cost you valuable opportunities.

These challenges clearly show why a new approach to strategy, planning, and analytics is beneficial and necessary for today's businesses. In the next section, we'll explore how artificial intelligence offers an answer to these challenges.

Enter Artificial Intelligence

Artificial Intelligence, with its subset of machine learning, catalyzes strategy, planning, and analytics. Imagine having a tireless virtual assistant who takes over the labor-intensive tasks of data collection and organization, freeing you up to focus on the strategic aspects of your business.

This isn't some distant future fantasy; this is the power of AI today. Let us break down how AI revolutionizes each step of the strategic planning process:

Automated Data Collection and Organization: AI can handle copious amounts of structured and unstructured data from multiple sources, collecting and organizing it efficiently. No more manual data entry into sprawling spreadsheets. AI does the groundwork for you, reducing human error and allowing you to handle larger volumes of data than ever before.

Advanced Data Analysis: Machine Learning algorithms can sift through complex datasets at lightning speed. They can uncover patterns and trends that are invisible to the naked eye. Think of it as having an eagle-eyed data scientist who never sleeps, constantly analyzing your data to deliver actionable insights.

Predictive Analytics: AI goes beyond just analyzing historical data. It can predict future trends based on current data, helping you forecast sales, market changes, and customer behavior. This gives you a crystal ball, allowing you to foresee opportunities and threats and make proactive decisions.

Data-Driven Decision-Making: AI's advanced analytics provide objective, data-driven insights, minimizing the reliance on human intuition and bias. It offers quantitative backing to your qualitative decisions, making your strategic moves more robust, accurate, and effective.

Real-Time Insights and Responses: AI tools can deliver real-time insights, enabling you to respond rapidly to market changes. With AI, your business can be as agile and adaptable as a startup, regardless of size.

AI offers a solution to the challenges the conventional approach faces through these capabilities. It makes the process more efficient, accurate, and scalable, enabling you to base your strategy on deep, data-driven insights.

Real-Life Example:
Netflix: The AI-Powered Entertainment Behemoth

Picture this: You're settling for a cozy evening at home, ready to dive into a new series or movie. You open Netflix, and there it is—a list of recommendations that read your mind, perfectly matching your preferences. This isn't magic but is the result of Netflix's sophisticated use of AI and machine learning.

Netflix's AI algorithms analyze vast amounts of user data, learning from each interaction to provide personalized movie recommendations. It's not just about suggesting what to watch next; Netflix uses AI to optimize streaming quality and even personalize movie thumbnails based on user preferences.

This AI-powered approach has proven beneficial for Netflix's advertising campaigns, as it accurately anticipates user movie preferences, potentially boosting subscriber numbers and user satisfaction.

By understanding what content resonates with viewers, Netflix can make informed decisions about where to allocate resources. Shows predicted to do well might receive more marketing budget or be renewed for additional seasons. This use of AI for resource allocation can be mirrored in your business to ensure that you're investing your resources in areas where they'll have the most impact.

Integrating AI Into Your Strategic Planning

Integrating AI into your strategic planning process can seem daunting, but it doesn't have to be. Here are some steps to get you started:

- **Identify Your Needs:** Identify areas where AI can add the most value. This could be data collection, analysis, predictive analytics, or decision-making. Once you've identified your needs, you can look for AI tools that address these areas.
- **Choose the Right Tools:** Many AI tools are available, each with strengths and weaknesses. Do your research to find the tools that best meet your needs. Some popular AI tools for strategic planning include Tableau for data visualization, RapidMiner for data analysis, and Salesforce Einstein for predictive analytics.

- **Train Your Team:** Implementing AI tools will require some training. Make sure your team understands how to use the tools and how they can benefit from them. This will ensure your team is on board with the changes and ready to make the most of the new tools.
- **Start Small:** You don't have to overhaul your entire strategic planning process at once. Start by implementing AI in one area; once you're comfortable with that, you can expand to other areas.
- **Measure and Adjust:** Once you've implemented AI, measure its impact. Ask yourself: Are you getting the insights you need? Is it saving you time? Is it improving your decision-making? Use these insights to adjust your approach and make the most of AI.

AI-Powered Planning and Analytics

Stage Name	Stage Description	What Happens	How AI Can Help	Example AI Tools
Data Collection	Initial Phase	Collection of raw data from various sources	AI can automate the process of data collection from diverse sources, ensuring accuracy and efficiency	Import.io, Mozenda
Data Cleaning	Pre-processing Stage	The process of detecting and correcting corrupt or inaccurate records from a dataset	AI can automate data cleaning, improving the quality and reliability of the data	Express Analytics, IBM Infosphere
Data Analysis	Processing Stage	Applying statistical and logical techniques to describe and illustrate, condense and recap, and evaluate data	AI can automate and enhance data analysis, offering predictive insights and identifying trends	RapidMiner, KNIME, Tableau AI

Decision Making	Strategic Stage	Process of making decisions based on the analyzed data	AI can provide decision-making support using predictive analytics and decision trees	Ginimachine, Rationale AI
Planning & Forecasting	Planning Stage	Using analyzed data to plan future business strategies and forecast trends	AI can help in scenario planning, forecasting trends, and anticipating customer behavior	Akkio, Peak AI
Monitoring & Control	Final Stage	Constant monitoring and controlling of strategies for effectiveness	AI can automate real-time monitoring and generate alerts for any discrepancies	Functionize, Tellius

Live Case Study:
Harnessing AI for Business Planning, Analytics and Strategy

Figure 24 - Techmart Store Image Generated by AI
(Source: Midjourney)

Context: Meet Jason, a diligent and forward-thinking business analyst at TechMart, a popular supermarket chain in the heart of San Francisco. As part of his role, Jason routinely assesses the supermarket's sales data to understand patterns and trends and to provide strategic recommendations to the management. Due to an urgent management meeting, Jason has been tasked to review the Sales data and make recommendations on the company's revenue and profit optimization, growth opportunities, and key focus areas for the upcoming year.

⚒ **AI tools used:**

- ChatGPT Code Interpreter (For analysis and strategic recommendations)

- Gamma App (For presentation)
- Microsoft Excel (Analyze functionality for further analysis and data visualization, where needed)
- Numerous AI (For building generative AI capability within Excel)

💡 Step-by-Step Playbook

Let's walk through Jason's AI-enhanced process to understand how AI can transform traditional business planning, analytics, and strategy roles.

<u>Step 1: Gathering and Cleaning Data</u>

Jason began by extracting the sales data for the past year from TehcMart's Point of Sale (POS) system into an Excel spreadsheet. He cleaned and prepared the data leveraging **Numerous AI**, addressing any outliers or discrepancies to avoid skewing the results.

<u>Step 2: Uploading Data into the AI System</u>

Next, Jason uploaded the cleaned data into the **ChatGPT code interpreter**. The interpreter was designed to understand and analyze complex datasets, making it a powerful tool for his task.

💡 *Note: Review the data submitted by Jason to ChatGPT in our online resource kit.*

<u>Step 3: Problem Solving Framework</u>

Knowing that some consultants are attending the management meeting, Jason asked **ChatGPT** to put on an expert analyst hat and deploy McKinsey's 7-Step Problem Solving Framework while analyzing data and making recommendations.

Sample Prompt from Jason: Can you act as an expert who has worked at large consultancy firms and is a pro at using McKinsey's 7-step problem-solving framework? You are tasked with analyzing this data and providing a step-by-step analysis based on the 7-step McKinsey framework. Use models and visuals to make it a comprehensive research and recommendation.

CHATGPT: Understood. The 7-step problem-solving framework consists of the following stages, which we will deploy as we analyze and make recommendations.

1. **Problem Definition**: Clearly define the problem.
2. **Problem Disaggregation**: Break down the problem into manageable parts.
3. **Prioritization**: Prioritize the issues to focus on based on impact and feasibility.
4. **Work Plan**: Define the approach to solve the problem.
5. **Analysis**: Analyze the situation using data and logic.
6. **Synthesis**: Integrate the findings into a coherent whole.
7. **Storyline**: Compellingly communicate the results.

Before he proceeded, Jason prompted ChatGPT to summarize the data to confirm that the AI had interpreted it correctly. This step was crucial to avoid misinterpretations leading to incorrect insights or recommendations.

Step 4: Uncovering Insights

Jason then asked **ChatGPT** to analyze the data and present critical insights. The AI combed through the extensive sales data, recognizing patterns and identifying trends that might take time to be visible to a human analyst.

ChatGPT summarized the analysis both in a data-backed and visual manner, calling out the price, profitability and average units per order spread, top products, regional spread, profitability stack, Key customer segments, order priority buckets, promotional discount cuts, and much more, at just a click of a button!

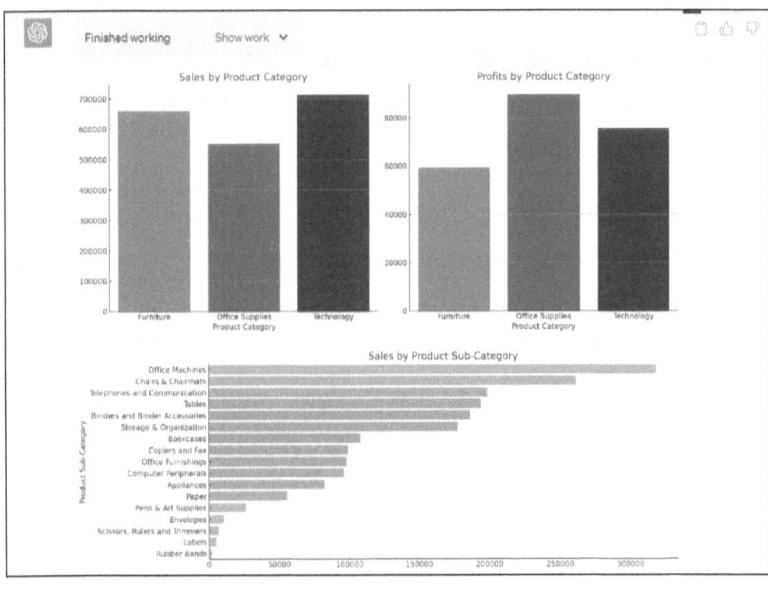

Figure 25 - Sample Visual Insights Generated By ChatGPT

Step 5: Generating Strategic Recommendations

After obtaining insights, Jason tasked **ChatGPT** with formulating strategic recommendations based on the findings, proofreading the results, and applying his expertise to complement the AI outputs. The AI used its deep learning capabilities to suggest impactful and feasible strategies that TechMart could implement.

Jason understood from the recommendations about opportunities related to focusing on high-selling and profitable products, reviewing the inventory risk in SLOB (slow moving and obsolete) products which can be actioned, regional nuances, customer segments, promotional strategies, shipping mode optimization, order priority mix, etc. in a particular manner, helping him get to the root cause faster.

With further follow-ups, ChatGPT also helped Jason put together frameworks like 2X2 Matrix summarizing the category and market attractiveness for investment decisions. This helped ingest a visually impactful narrative in the recommendations.

💡**Note:** Refer to our online resource for more detailed output generated with AI.

Step 6: Summarizing Recommendations

Finally, Jason prompted **ChatGPT** to distill the list of recommendations into the top three most impactful actions TechMart can take. This made it easier for the management to prioritize and make informed decisions.

CHATGPT: Based on the detailed analysis of your sales data, here are the top three recommendations that could be highlighted in your final slide.

1. **Focus on Profitable Segments and Products**: The 'Home Office' customer segment and the 'Office Supplies' product category showed the highest profitability. Consider tailoring marketing strategies to target this customer segment and promoting products from this category. Additionally, focus on the high-selling and profitable products such as 'The Fellowes

PB500 Electric Punch Plastic Comb Binding Machine with Manual Bind' and 'Lexmark 4227 Plus Dot Matrix Printer.'
2. **Review Regional Strategies**: The sales and quantity sold are highest in the East region and lowest in the South. Applying successful strategies from the East region to the other areas might be beneficial. Also, investigate the reasons for lower sales in the South region and consider implementing strategies to boost performance there.
3. **Optimize Pricing and Discount Strategies**: The analysis showed that high order priority or discounts do not necessarily lead to increased sales or profits. Consider reviewing your pricing and discount strategies to ensure they are leading to profitable sales. For instance, reducing discounts on less profitable items and offering targeted discounts on more profitable or slow-moving items might lead to better results.

Through this method, Jason effectively leverages AI to analyze large amounts of data and derive actionable insights and recommendations, significantly improving the supermarket's strategic planning and decision-making process.

This is just a sample output for the AI tool to showcase the power of using AI at work. We could make this more sophisticated and detailed in a real-life scenario and imagine the benefit in various areas like sales, where our team can save time from research and spend it productively in more partner or customer-facing conversations!

Step 7: Compiling a Presentation with Gamma AI

With the top recommendations, Jason presented his findings and suggestions to the management. To do this, he employed **Gamma**

App, an AI tool that assisted him in creating a professional presentation. He input key callouts, and Gamma automatically generated a comprehensive, visually appealing slide deck. This AI-powered tool saved Jason hours of manual work and ensured a well-structured, impactful presentation.

This case study illustrates how AI can seamlessly integrate into traditional business roles, improving efficiency and accuracy.

Thanks to AI, the entire process from data collection to a board-ready presentation is reduced by 10x, providing Jason (and Techmart) with rapid, actionable strategies. This is a simple illustration to help you understand the power of utilizing AI for business analysis and strategic decision-making. AI doesn't replace our efforts but enhances them, making us 10x more efficient and faster!

AI AND THE TRANSFORMATION OF SUPPLY CHAIN MANAGEMENT

"Supply chains cannot tolerate even 24 hours of disruption. So if you lose your place in the supply chain because of wild behavior, you could lose a lot."
— *Thomas Friedman*

*L*et's rewind to my time as the country manager for a consumer organization. My role involved managing the entire spectrum of country operations, including various supply chain activities—from sourcing to manufacturing, logistics to quality assurance, and demand forecasting to inventory management. It was a colossal task, with numerous moving parts that required simultaneous attention.

We had over 100 stock-keeping units (SKUs), each with its unique raw materials and packaging set. This translated into almost 10,000 individual items to manage regarding sourcing and planning. Any lapse in planning could lead to a domino effect of consequences—overproduction could result in obsolete inventory, while underproduction could lead to lost sales.

We had to strategize optimal buffer inventories, identify manufacturing defects early, accelerate production processes where possible, and optimize the layout for our stored items.

The challenges continued. The aim was to lower manufacturing costs while enhancing output and speed. We had to devise effective plans for distribution for our distributors and retailers. We were tasked with managing delivery routes to ensure fast yet cost-efficient distribution. The operation was complex and exhaustive, from sourcing the suitable raw materials and packaging to delivering the final product to the right place, at the right time, at the correct cost.

While we did have ERP systems in place, the manual involvement across the supply chain was considerable. I often wondered if there was a way to make the entire process 10 times more efficient, quicker, and automated.

Fast forward to the present, and it's exhilarating to see how AI tools can do just that; they can streamline, enhance, and automate the entire supply chain process. AI revolutionizes supply chain management by driving efficiencies, speed, and automation. This chapter will explore how these AI tools can transform your supply chain, making it a powerful engine for your business growth. Get ready for a thrilling exploration of AI and the transformation of supply chain management.

The Conventional Way and its Shortcomings

In the traditional realm of supply chain management, a myriad of intricate processes intertwine from the very inception, where sourcing raw materials is the prime focus, to the endpoint, where the consumer finally receives the finished goods. This long-winded product lifecycle journey is punctuated with multiple stages, including manufacturing, inventory management, warehouse organization, vendor relationship management, demand forecasting, logistics, and transportation.

Traditionally, a combination of software systems and manual intervention has been employed to navigate through these processes. While this has served its purpose to an extent, there have been noticeable areas for improvement.

Demand Forecasting: A crucial part of supply chain management, demand forecasting has conventionally relied on the study of historical data and educated predictions. This method, however rudimentary, provides a baseline for planning. However, the limitation of this approach becomes glaringly evident when the future fails to emulate the past. Factors such as rapidly shifting consumer behavior, dynamic market trends, or unforeseen circumstances like a pandemic can throw these predictions off track, leading to inventory surplus or shortfall.

Vendor Relationships and Contracts: Cultivating relationships with vendors and handling contracts requires significant time and human resources. The conventional way often involves manual contract creation, review, and management processes. These labor-intensive tasks can lead to errors, oversights, legal complications, and strained vendor relationships.

Quality Control: Ensuring the quality of products throughout the supply chain is a critical task. Traditional methods typically involve human inspection and manual quality checks. These methods, while effective to a degree, are not foolproof and can miss subtle defects. Furthermore, as the scale of production increases, maintaining consistent quality control through manual processes becomes increasingly challenging.

Inventory Management and Logistics: Keeping track of inventory levels in real-time, coordinating the movement of goods, planning optimal routes, and scheduling deliveries are all components of supply chain management that traditionally have required extensive human effort. Manual processes can lead to inefficiencies, inaccuracies, and delays.

Manufacturing: The traditional manufacturing process involves a series of steps, from planning and procurement to assembly and inspection. These steps are often carried out manually or with the help of basic automation tools, leading to potential errors, inefficiencies, and inconsistencies. Furthermore, the lack of real-time data and predictive capabilities can result in production delays, quality issues, and increased costs.

Returns and After-Sales Services: Managing returns and providing after-sales services is critical to supply chain management. Traditional methods often involve manual processes to handle returns, process refunds, manage warranties, and provide customer support. These methods can be labor-intensive, slow, and prone to errors, leading to customer dissatisfaction and potential loss of business.

Sustainability: In the traditional supply chain, sustainability is often an afterthought, with little emphasis on reducing waste, minimizing carbon footprint, or promoting ethical sourcing and fair trade practices. This lack of focus on sustainability can lead to environmental harm, damage to the company's reputation, and potential regulatory penalties.

The cumulative impact of these challenges is that traditional supply chain management can be cost and time-intensive, often requiring significant resources. There's a constant struggle to balance operational efficiency and cost optimization.

In these challenges, supply chain management is ripe for a transformation. It calls for a solution that can minimize the reliance on guesswork, automate manual tasks, streamline operations, and make the process more efficient and cost-effective. This is where artificial intelligence comes in.

The AI Revolution in Supply Chain Management

Artificial intelligence (AI) is poised to revolutionize supply chain management. With its ability to process vast amounts of data, make accurate predictions, automate complex processes, and learn from past patterns, AI is set to transform the traditional supply chain landscape.

Demand Forecasting: AI elevates demand forecasting from a speculative exercise to a precise science. AI can generate accurate demand predictions by analyzing real-time data from diverse sources, including sales data, market trends, weather patterns, and social media sentiment. This leads to optimized inventory levels, reducing waste and overhead costs. Moreover, it ensures the constant availability of products, enhancing customer satisfaction and loyalty.

Vendor Relationships and Contracts: AI can streamline the management of contracts and vendor relationships, have traditionally been complex and manual processes. AI-powered tools can scrutinize contract terms, monitor vendor performance, and highlight potential issues, reducing the scope for human error and fostering healthier, more productive vendor relationships.

Quality Control: AI can significantly enhance quality control processes. AI-powered visual inspection tools can detect defects and inconsistencies with accuracy that surpasses human capabilities. This ensures that only high-quality products reach the market, enhancing brand reputation and customer satisfaction.

Manufacturing: AI can optimize the manufacturing process by predicting production needs based on demand forecasts, identifying potential bottlenecks, and suggesting process improvements. This can lead to increased production efficiency, reduced waste, and cost savings.

Returns and After-Sales Services: AI can streamline the management of returns and after-sales services. AI-powered tools can automate the processing of returns, manage warranties, and provide personalized customer support, improving customer satisfaction and loyalty.

Sustainability: AI can help companies make their supply chains more sustainable. AI can help companies reduce their environmental impact and meet their sustainability goals by optimizing resource usage, reducing waste, and promoting ethical sourcing practices.

Cost and Time Efficiency: By automating routine tasks, optimizing processes, and providing real-time insights, AI can significantly reduce the time and cost associated with supply chain management. This allows companies to allocate resources more effectively, focusing on strategic decision-making and innovation.

In essence, AI has the potential to transform supply chains into more efficient, resilient, and customer-centric operations. By integrating AI into supply chain management, companies can enhance operational efficiency, improve accuracy, generate cost savings, and increase customer satisfaction. This marks the dawn of a new era in supply chain management powered by AI.

Real-Life Example:

Amazon: Harnessing AI to Revolutionize Supply Chain and Delivery

Imagine ordering a product on Amazon and having it delivered to your doorstep the very next day or even on the same day. A powerful force lies behind this impressive speed and efficiency: Amazon uses artificial intelligence (AI) in its supply chain and delivery processes.

Amazon, the world's largest online retailer, has prioritized the use of AI to accelerate its delivery services and minimize the distance traveled.

One key area where AI plays a pivotal role is in transportation, particularly in mapping and planning routes while considering variations. AI algorithms analyze vast amounts of data to devise the most efficient routes, ensuring that packages reach customers as quickly as possible.

Another critical aspect is inventory management. With Amazon's vast array of products, deciding where to place an inventory unit is a complex task. AI comes into play here, analyzing data and trends to determine the optimal location for each inventory unit. By positioning inventory closer to customers, Amazon can reduce delivery times and offer same-day or next-day delivery services, akin to the service provided by its Prime membership program.

Amazon's use of AI extends to its fulfillment centers as well. The company uses robotics, powered by AI, to assist with repetitive tasks such as lifting heavy items. According to the company, automation handles 75% of Amazon customer orders, significantly enhancing efficiency and speed.

The company's recent initiative, Amazon Anywhere, further exemplifies the innovative use of AI. This new immersive shopping experience allows customers to purchase physical items within games and mobile apps, bringing Amazon's online commerce into the realm of video games and smartphone applications.

However, the integration of AI also presents challenges. Ensuring data privacy and managing the impact on employment are key considerations. Amazon must also continuously innovate to stay ahead of the competition and meet the ever-evolving customer expectations.

Despite these challenges, Amazon's use of AI in its supply chain and delivery processes is a testament to the transformative power of this technology. It showcases how AI can revolutionize business operations, enhance customer experience, and provide a competitive edge in today's digital age. Amazon's AI journey serves as a shining example for businesses worldwide, demonstrating how AI can drive innovation, efficiency, and growth.

Integration of AI Across the Supply Chain Funnel

The supply chain funnel represents the journey of a product from its raw material stage to its final delivery to the customer. This journey comprises several stages, each with unique challenges and opportunities. AI can be integrated across this funnel to streamline processes, enhance efficiency, and drive growth. Let's explore how:

- **Sourcing and Procurement:** AI can analyze vast amounts of data from various sources to identify the best suppliers, negotiate optimal prices, and manage contracts. Machine learning algorithms can predict supplier performance based on historical data, helping businesses to make more informed decisions. AI can also automate routine tasks such as order placement and invoice processing, freeing up procurement teams to focus on strategic tasks.
- **Production and Manufacturing:** AI can optimize production schedules based on real-time demand forecasts, reducing waste

and improving efficiency. Machine learning algorithms can identify patterns in production data to predict and prevent equipment failures, reducing downtime. AI-powered visual inspection systems can also enhance quality control by detecting defects that human inspectors might miss.

- **Inventory Management:** AI can predict future demand trends, helping businesses optimize inventory levels. This can prevent overstocking and understocking scenarios, reducing storage costs and improving customer satisfaction. AI can also automate routine tasks such as stock counting and reordering, saving time and reducing the risk of human error.
- **Logistics and Distribution:** AI can optimize delivery routes, considering traffic conditions, weather forecasts, and delivery schedules. This can reduce fuel costs, improve delivery times, and enhance customer satisfaction. AI can also predict potential disruptions in the supply chain and provide alternative solutions, improving resilience.
- **Customer Service:** AI can enhance the customer experience by providing personalized product recommendations, improving delivery tracking, and automating customer service interactions. Machine learning algorithms can analyze customer behavior and feedback to identify trends and opportunities for improvement.

Integrating AI across the supply chain funnel allows businesses to transform their operations from disconnected stages into a cohesive, efficient, and customer-centric process. This can drive significant improvements in efficiency, cost-effectiveness, and customer satisfaction, giving businesses a competitive edge in today's fast-paced and dynamic market.

AI-Powered Supply Chain Framework

Stage Name	Stage Description	What Happens	How AI Can Help	Example AI Tools
Demand Forecasting	Predicting the Demand	Estimating the quantity of a product or service that consumers will purchase	AI can help by accurately predicting demand using historical sales data, market trends, and other influencing factors	IBM Watson Supply Chain Insights, Peak.ai
Procurement	Purchasing Stage	The process of finding and acquiring goods and services from external sources	Predictive analytics can be used for demand and supply forecasting to make smart procurement decisions	Sievo, Keelvar
Production	Manufacturing Stage	Converting raw materials into finished goods	Quality control automation, process optimization, and predictive maintenance with AI	Machina Labs, Bright Machines

	Stage	Description	AI Application	Examples
Storage	Warehouse Stage	The storing of goods before they are sold	AI can optimize inventory management by predicting what will be needed, where, and when	Logiwa, Cyzerg
Distribution	Delivery Stage	Moving the goods from the point of production to the point of consumption	AI can optimize route planning, delivery scheduling and track shipments in real time	Locus, Route4Me
Customer Service	After Sales Stage	Interacting with customers to handle their queries and complaints	AI chatbots can provide 24/7 customer support; predictive analytics can be used for predictive maintenance	Zendesk, Intercom
Returns and After-sales Service	Post-Purchase Stage	Managing returns, repairs, and maintenance of products	AI can automate returns processing and use predictive analytics for proactive after-sales service	Returnly, GardxEngage

Live Case Study
AI-Powered Supply Chain Management

Figure 26 - Creative Technology Factory Image Generated by AI (Source: Midjourney)

Context: Meet Amanda, the dynamic head of supply chain at Creative Technology, a leading healthcare company specializing in innovative medical devices. Amanda's role requires her to manage the company's global supply chain operations. The complexities and uncertainties in the modern supply chain, especially in light of the COVID-19 pandemic, have made predictive analytics a pivotal tool. To ensure the company meets its supply chain objectives and is prepared for unforeseen disruptions, Amanda aims to harness the power of AI, integrating it into the process.

🛠 AI tools used:

ChatGPT Code Interpreter (For supply chain analysis and recommendations)

Akkio (For predictive analysis, data transformation, and visualization)

Google Sheets (For data maintenance and collaborative analysis)

Numerous AI (For activating generative AI capabilities within excel)

Zapier (For automating tasks and integrating different software tools)

Slack (For team communication and real-time alerts)

💡 Step-by-Step Playbook

Step 1: Gathering and Organizing Data

Amanda collected supply chain data from Creative Technology's ERP system. She organized this data as tasks in Google Sheets powered with **Numerous AI** plugin, ensuring data accuracy and consistency.

Step 2: Setting Up Automation with Zapier

Amanda used **Zapier** for real-time data updates and team communication:

Alerts were automatically sent via Slack whenever there were changes in the Google Sheets data. Automated tasks initiated alternative plans when there was a constraint or block in the process and informed stakeholders about delays or supply chain disruptions.

Step 3: Data Transformation with Akkio

Before delving into deep analysis, Amanda used **Akkio** to transform and visualize the data. Akkio's intuitive interface allowed her to effortlessly clean data, reformat dates, combine columns, and remove outliers, ensuring the data is primed for analysis.

Step 4: Predictive Analysis using Akkio

Amanda leveraged **Akkio**'s machine learning capabilities to predict potential supply chain disruptions, forecast demand, and identify potential bottlenecks. Akkio's AutoML feature ensured that best-in-class models were generated swiftly, allowing Amanda to make data-driven decisions efficiently.

Step 5: Deep Dive Analysis with ChatGPT

Amanda uploaded the structured data into the **ChatGPT** code interpreter for more granular insights. She sought insights into the supply chain's efficiency and areas of improvement.

Sample prompt from Amanda: "Analyze this data, focusing on lean supply chain management principles, and provide insights to make our supply chain more agile and resilient."

ChatGPT analyzed the data using lean principles and provided insights on waste reduction, just-in-time inventory, and supplier relationship optimization.

Step 6: Communication and Collaboration

Amanda collaborated with her team on **Slack**, which serves as a platform for team communication and as a real-time alert system, ensuring that insights from the AI analysis were immediately shared with the relevant stakeholders.

Step 7: Strategic Recommendations

Amanda tasked **ChatGPT** with crafting strategic recommendations to elevate the supply chain. It suggested diversifying the supplier base, implementing predictive analytics for demand forecasting, optimizing inventory management, and enhancing end-to-end visibility.

Step 8: Decision Making and Implementation

Having gathered insights and recommendations, Amanda discussed them with her team on Slack. They prioritized actions and delegated responsibilities. Using Google Sheets, Zapier, and Slack, they monitor the recommendations' implementation and their impact on the supply chain.

Amanda's integration of AI tools like ChatGPT, Akkio, Google Sheets, Zapier, and Slack into Creative Technology's supply chain management revolutionized their operations. This proactive approach made the process more efficient, agile and also more resilient to external disruptions. By leveraging these cutting-edge tools, Amanda established a gold standard for modern supply chain management in the healthcare sector, ensuring Creative Technology remained at the forefront of innovation.

The following section will dive into our ninth AI plug-and-play strategy: customer service and support. Ready to keep going?

REVOLUTIONIZING CUSTOMER EXPERIENCE AND SUPPORT WITH AI

> *"The purpose of a business is to create a customer who creates customers."*
> *— Shiv Singh*

Take a journey back in time with me to an earlier role where I was tasked with launching and scaling up a luxury skincare brand. In this high-stakes, high-expectations context, customer experience and support were the cornerstones of our brand success. We were catering to an elite clientele that demanded exceptional service, and meeting their expectations was a complex dance involving multiple facets of our business.

Imagine the intricacies of designing appealing kiosks and stores, meticulously crafting their layout and product placements, and training our staff to engage impeccably with customers. Picture the challenge of creating a high-conversion, impactful website that provides a seamless, conversational customer journey. In this space, live customer engagements were necessary but hard to achieve, given our lean team.

Consider the strategic importance of continually gathering customer feedback to enhance our product portfolio. The idea of co-creating products with our customers was exciting and daunting, an initiative that promised new business development opportunities but required an open channel for constant communication.

We knew the value of fostering customer trust and loyalty, so we rolled out a comprehensive loyalty program. This program aimed to understand our customers' buying patterns, recommend suitable products, incentivize their interactions with our brand, and foster opportunities to cross-sell and upsell our offerings. Our promotional campaigns were an integral part of this immersive customer experience.

Yes, we scaled the brand and succeeded in our target market. Yet, reflecting on that journey, I recognize how much time, energy, and resources we devoted to reaching that milestone. The entire process could have been 10x more efficient, faster, and ROI-friendly had we been able to automate some core processes and enrich our customer support and experience strategy.

Today, the game has changed dramatically. Thanks to AI tools, tasks that once required an entire team's effort can be handled effectively, even by a solo entrepreneur. AI's power to enhance customer experience and support is immense. It allows us to offer a more elevated, engaging service while improving efficiency and speed. In this chapter, we'll explore how to harness the revolutionary power of AI to redefine customer experience and support for your business.

The Conventional Way and its Shortcomings

Let's step back and imagine ourselves in a scenario where we need immediate assistance with a product or service. Whether it's understanding how to use a new feature, solving a sudden technical glitch, or seeking answers to billing queries - the first point of contact is usually customer support. In a traditional setup, you might pick up the phone, navigate through a complicated IVR system, and finally reach a human agent who can assist you.

Now, here is where the challenges begin. Firstly, customer service representatives are humans, after all. They have their schedules, limitations, and working hours. 24/7 support is more of a luxury than a norm in the traditional setup. Even in companies that offer round-the-clock service, the off-hours support might be skeleton staff, meaning longer wait times and potential delays in resolving your issue.

Secondly, human agents can only handle one customer at a time. Even the most efficient customer service representative has a limit to how many customers they can assist in a day. This often results in customers being put on hold, especially during peak hours, which leads to frustration and dissatisfaction.

Thirdly, there's a potential for inconsistency. Different agents handle the same issue differently based on their interpretation, understanding, and experience. This can lead to an inconsistent customer experience, with some customers resolving their issues quickly and others going through lengthy processes for the same problem.

Finally, there's the challenge of scalability. As the business expands and the number of customers grows, the number of customer service requests grows, too. Scaling a human-based customer support team is more than just expensive. It requires substantial time and resources for recruitment, training, and management.

While the human touch in customer service is irreplaceable, the traditional approach poses significant challenges that can hinder a business's growth and ability to provide an excellent customer experience. But what if there's a way to combine the best of both worlds—the efficiency and scalability of technology with the personal touch of human service? That's where Artificial Intelligence enters the picture.

Enter Artificial Intelligence and Benefits of Implementation

Imagine a world where human limitations no longer bind customer support and are equipped with artificial intelligence's power. In this transformed landscape, AI doesn't replace the human touch but amplifies it, ensuring efficiency, consistency, and personalized service while being available round-the-clock. Here's how AI breathes new life into customer experience and customer support:

Efficiency on Steroids: AI-powered tools like chatbots and virtual assistants can handle multiple customer interactions simultaneously, offering immediate responses and significantly reducing wait times. Unlike humans, these digital assistants don't tire or need breaks, and their attention to detail remains consistent regardless of the number of queries they handle. The result? Customers get instant assistance, and the efficiency of customer service skyrockets.

Consistency is Key: In customer service, how you handle customers can determine if they will return or not as loyal customers. AI-powered systems can be programmed to provide consistent responses to similar queries, ensuring every customer gets the same high-quality experience. Machine learning algorithms enable these systems to learn from past interactions, continuously improving their performance over time.

Seamless Scalability: As your business grows, so does the volume of customer interactions. With traditional customer service, scaling to match this growing demand can take time and effort. However, with AI, scaling becomes as simple as upgrading your software. AI solutions can easily handle increased customer interactions without the need for proportional cost increases.

24/7 Support: Unlike human agents, AI doesn't sleep, doesn't need weekends off, and doesn't take vacations. AI-powered customer support can be available all day and night, offering instant assistance whenever a customer reaches out. This round-the-clock availability benefits businesses operating across different time zones, ensuring every customer is on time.

Personalized Service: Personalization is the secret ingredient for an exceptional customer experience. With its ability to quickly analyze vast amounts of data, AI can provide insights into individual customer preferences, behavior, and history. This information can tailor customer interactions and support, providing personalized recommendations and solutions and making customers feel valued and understood.

In summary, integrating AI in customer service serves as a game-changer, offering businesses an opportunity to overcome traditional hurdles and deliver an unparalleled customer experience.

Real-Life Example:
Nike: The Perfect Blend of Sports and AI

As you lace up your Nike shoes for a morning run or slip into your favorite Nike sports gear, there's more to your Nike experience than meets the eye. Behind the scenes, Nike's AI-driven customer experience machinery ensures that your interaction with the brand is as personalized and engaging as possible.

Nike's AI journey began with acquiring several tech companies, integrating AI and computer vision into their apps. This strategic move allowed Nike to focus on customer connection, improving business longevity, and direct sales strategies.

One of the most innovative applications of AI is the "Nike Maker Experience," which employs AI for instant sneaker customization. Imagine walking into a Nike store and walking out with a pair of sneakers designed exclusively for you, all within less than an hour. That's the power of AI at work.

But the AI magic doesn't stop at the store. Nike's "Nike+" program offers its members personalized relationships and exclusive benefits. And when it comes to finding the perfect shoe size, the

"Nike Fit" app uses AI elements to ensure a precise fit, enhancing customer satisfaction.

Nike's AI strategy also extends to its virtual assistants. These AI-powered assistants provide customers with delightful experiences, answer queries, offer recommendations, and even help with purchases. This seamless integration of AI into customer service enhances customer engagement and leads to growth.

As you lace up your Nike shoes for your next run, remember that it's not just a pair of shoes you're wearing. It's a product of a brand harnessing AI's power to redefine customer engagement and personalization. It's a testament to the incredible power of AI in transforming the world of branding and marketing.

AI Integration Across Customer Service and Experience

AI can be integrated across various facets of customer service and experience to drive efficiency, personalization, and customer satisfaction. Here's how:

- **Customer Support**: AI-powered chatbots and virtual assistants can handle many customer queries simultaneously, providing instant responses and reducing wait times. They can be programmed to provide consistent responses, ensuring a uniform customer experience. Furthermore, machine learning enables these systems to learn from past interactions and improve their performance over time.
- **Personalized Experience**: AI can analyze vast amounts of data to gain insights into customer preferences, behavior, and history. This information can personalize customer interactions,

product recommendations, and marketing messages, making customers feel valued and understood.

- **Predictive Analysis**: AI can predict future customer behavior based on past interactions and other data. This can help businesses anticipate customer needs, improve product recommendations, and proactively address potential issues, enhancing the overall customer experience.
- **Real-Time Assistance**: AI can provide real-time assistance to customers, helping them navigate websites, answering product queries, and even assisting with checkouts. This can significantly enhance the online shopping experience and increase conversion rates.
- **Feedback Analysis**: AI can analyze customer feedback from various sources, including surveys, social media, and online reviews, to identify common themes and areas for improvement. This can provide valuable insights to help businesses improve their products, services, and overall customer experience.
- **Automated Processes**: AI can automate routine tasks such as order tracking, appointment scheduling, and invoice generation, freeing human staff to focus on more complex customer service tasks.

Integrating AI across these areas can provide a seamless, personalized customer experience, improve customer satisfaction, and drive business growth.

AI-Powered Customer Support

Stage Name	Stage Description	What Happens	How AI Can Help	Example AI Tools
Awareness	Early interaction	Potential customers become aware of your products or services	AI can personalize marketing content to make it more appealing and relevant	Marketo, HubSpot
Interest	Evaluation	Potential customers begin researching your offerings	AI-powered chatbots can provide instant assistance, guiding customers with product details	Drift, Intercom

Purchase	Decision-making	Customer decides to buy your product or service	AI can streamline the purchasing process, making it quicker and easier. It can also use predictive analytics for cross-selling and up-selling	Pecan AI, Salesforce Einstein
Post-Purchase Support	After-sales service	Customers might have questions or issues after purchase	AI-powered customer service bots can provide quick solutions, reducing wait time	Zendesk, Zoho Desk, Thankful
Loyalty & Advocacy	Long-term relationship	Happy customers become brand advocates	AI can analyze customer behavior and provide personalized offers to boost customer loyalty	Yotpo, Smile.io

Live Case Study
Leveraging AI In Customer Support and Experience

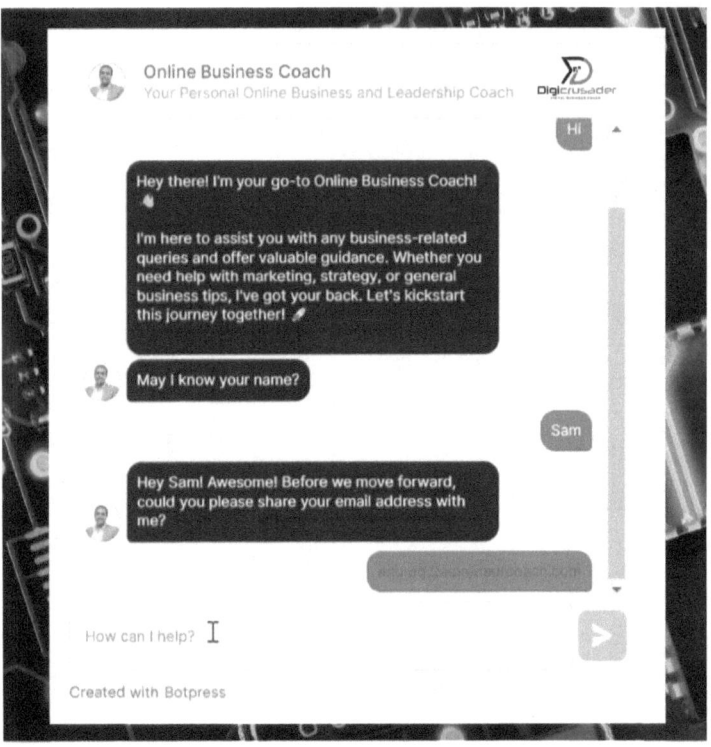

Figure 27 - Revolutionizing Customer Experience with AI at Digicrusader.com

Context: AJ, the founder of Digicrusader.com, an online business coaching platform, faced a challenge. His website was attracting a growing number of visitors. Still, he struggled to engage with them in a personalized way due to time constraints. Moreover, he wanted to continuously improve his site content based on customer feedback and create personalized responses based on what his target customers sought. To address these challenges, AJ decided to integrate AI tools into his customer support and experience strategy.

🛠 AI tools used:
- Botpress (For creating the chatbot)
- ChatGPT (For training chatbot with website content, persona, custom email creation...)
- Brevo (For email marketing as a CRM tool)
- Figma (For workflow ideation)
- Zapier (For automating the entire workflow)

💡 Step-by-Step Playbook

Step 1: Creating a Chatbot with Botpress

AJ started by creating a chatbot using **Botpress**, an open-source chatbot platform. He trained the chatbot with his own blog data and writing style, enabling it to interact with visitors in a manner consistent with his brand voice. This chatbot served as the first point of contact for visitors, answering common questions, providing information about AJ's coaching services, and conversationally engaging visitors.

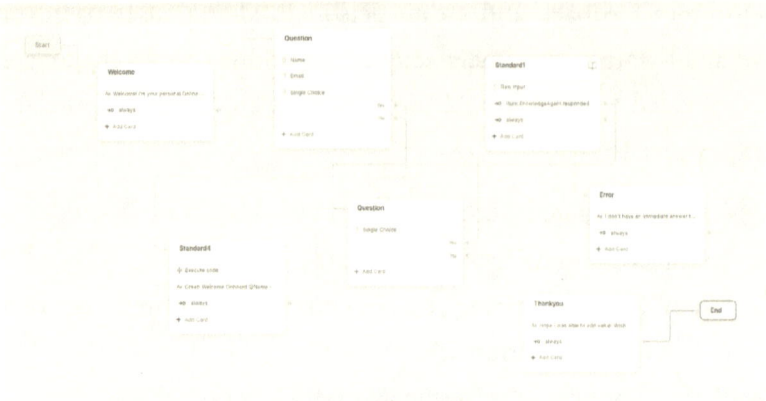

Figure 28 - Botpress No Code Chatbot Backend Design

Step 2: Integrating the Chatbot into the Website

Once the chatbot was ready, AJ integrated it into his website. This allowed visitors to interact with the chatbot directly from the website, enhancing their user experience. The chatbot was available 24/7, providing instant responses to visitor inquiries and ensuring no visitor was left waiting for a response.

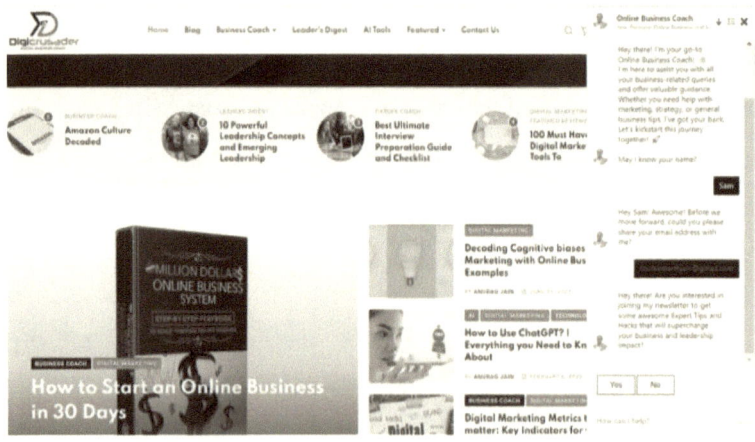

Figure 29 - Live AI-Powered Chat Interface on the Website

Step 3: Automating Subscriber Information Routing with Zapier

To manage his growing subscriber base, AJ used **Zapier**, an automation tool, to route subscriber information to his CRM tool, **Brevo**. Whenever a visitor subscribed to his newsletter or signed up for his coaching services, their information was automatically added to Brevo. This automation saved AJ time and ensured no subscriber information was lost or overlooked.

Step 4: Collecting Customer Feedback with Custom Survey Forms

AJ wanted to understand what his visitors were looking for on his website and what they could not find. To gather this information, he created a custom survey form asking visitors for their feedback. This form was integrated into the website and the chatbot, making it easy for visitors to provide feedback.

Step 5: Channeling Feedback to ChatGPT via Zapier

AJ used Zapier to channel the feedback from the survey forms to **ChatGPT**, a generative AI model. ChatGPT analyzed the feedback and generated personalized responses based on visitors'. This allowed AJ to address visitor inquiries and feedback in a personalized and efficient manner.

Step 6: Sending Personalized Responses to Customers

Once the personalized responses were generated, AJ used his CRM tool, Brevo, to send these responses to the customers via email. This ensured that each customer received a personalized response addressing their specific inquiry or feedback, enhancing their customer experience and making them feel valued.

Step 7: Achieving High Engagement and Conversion Rates

By integrating AI tools into his customer support and experience strategy, AJ was able to create a highly engaging and personalized experience for his visitors. This led to higher engagement rates, increased conversions, and a growing reader base. Moreover, this entire process was automated, allowing AJ to provide high-quality customer support and experience on autopilot.

AJ's case study demonstrates the transformative power of AI in customer support and experience. By leveraging AI tools, he enhanced his customer engagement, improved his site content based on customer feedback, and provided personalized responses to his customers. This not only improved his customer experience but also led to higher conversion rates and a growing reader base.

AJ's story demonstrates the power of AI, not just for big corporations but also for solopreneurs with limited resources. His journey shows that with the right tools, anyone can leverage AI to solve real-world problems and drive innovation.

In the next section, we will explore another exciting application of AI in business process automation. This is one of the core benefits of AI integration in business and a low-hanging fruit for entrepreneurs and leaders alike.

THE AI-DRIVEN BUSINESS PROCESS AUTOMATION

> *"The first rule of any technology used in a business is that automation applied to an efficient operation will magnify the efficiency. The second is that automation applied to an inefficient operation will magnify the inefficiency."*
> *– Bill Gates*

*W*elcome aboard the AI Express again! The journey that began with enhancing self as a leader has brought us across various facets of business where AI can be a game-changer. In this chapter, let's explore one of the most revolutionary aspects of AI applications in industry: Business Process Automation (BPA).

Let's travel back to when I was managing the operations of an entire country business, overseeing hundreds of team members in a vast and complex process. We had hundreds of stock-keeping units (SKUs) with raw materials and packaging components. This complexity multiplied into more than 10,000 individual items that needed to be managed, from sourcing to the final offtake from the shelf.

Consider the intricate dependencies, both internal and external. If a raw material's stock dwindles, an order must be placed with the vendor. If a retailer's inventory was low, the distributor had to initiate a reorder. Surplus stock may have languished at one retailer, necessitating a transfer to another retailer where sales are more robust. These instances required significant coordination between various functions and stakeholders, leading to an often overwhelming need for communication and follow-ups.

Imagine the kind of internal communication needed, too. For instance, if a distributor delayed payment, a salesperson needed to be alerted to follow up, and then the distributor needed to be reminded to settle the bills. Our team juggled such follow-ups continuously, upstream and downstream.

We did manage to scale the business significantly. Still, I can't help but wonder how much faster and more efficiently we could have grown without the constant exhaustion that came with manual operations. That's where the power of AI tools, readily available today, comes into play.

Imagine the possibilities of a tool like Zapier, capable of setting off a sequence of automated actions based on specific triggers. For instance, as a distributor nears a payment deadline, an automatic email could be triggered to the salesperson in charge of following up. Another AI, such as ChatGPT, could draft a personalized email and send it to the distributor via a CRM Tool, WhatsApp message, or any other preferred medium.

This automation of tasks and the potential for a seamless, closed-loop workflow without manual intervention is truly exciting. And this example barely scratches the surface. The possibility of automating our businesses, team workflows, and interactions with internal and external stakeholders is immense. AI has the power to drive unprecedented productivity enhancements. This chapter will explore how to tap into this potential and navigate the future of AI-driven business automation.

The Conventional Way

In the traditional business landscape, processes were primarily manual, relying heavily on human intervention at every step. Let's take a moment to reflect on the conventional approach to business process management:

Manual Data Entry and Management: Before the advent of sophisticated AI tools, data entry was tedious and often prone to human errors. Businesses rely on individuals to input data into systems, cross-check for discrepancies, and manage vast databases. This consumed a significant amount of time but also increased the chances of inaccuracies.

Reactive Approach: Traditional systems wait for problems to arise before addressing them. For instance, stock-outs would be noticed only when a customer order couldn't be fulfilled, leading to lost sales and dissatisfied customers.

Linear Workflows: Processes were often linear, with one task following another in a set sequence. If one task was delayed, the subsequent tasks would inevitably be affected, leading to bottlenecks and inefficiencies.

Limited Scalability: As businesses grew, the manual processes became even more cumbersome. Scaling operations often meant hiring more people, increasing costs and complexities.

Lack of Real-time Insights: Decision-making was often based on historical data rather than real-time insights. This reactive approach meant businesses were always a step behind, trying to catch up with market dynamics.

Dependency on Human Judgment: While human judgment is invaluable, relying solely on it without the support of data-driven insights can lead to biased or uninformed decisions. In the conventional setup, managers and leaders often had to make decisions based on gut feelings or limited data.

Communication Gaps: Communication was a significant challenge with multiple departments and stakeholders involved. Information often got lost in translation, leading to misaligned objectives and inefficiencies.

Cost Inefficiencies: Manual processes, especially repetitive and mundane tasks, were not only time-consuming but also cost-intensive. Businesses had to invest in resources for tasks that added little strategic value.

Reflecting on these challenges, it's evident that the conventional way, while functional, was riddled with inefficiencies, inaccuracies, and limitations. The need for a more streamlined, efficient, and intelligent approach was evident. This is where the promise of AI-driven business process automation comes into the picture, offering a paradigm shift in how businesses operate and thrive.

Enter Artificial Intelligence

As we exit the domain of conventional business process management, we find ourselves at the doorstep of a new era, one punctuated by the hum of artificial intelligence. This new paradigm of AI-driven business process automation is a game-changer, redefining the possibilities and potential of what we can achieve within our businesses. This is more than just a minor upgrade from the manual way of doing things. It's a transformative shift, and it's reshaping the very fabric of business operations.

In the AI era, those cumbersome manual tasks become streamlined and efficient. AI, with its ability to process huge amounts of data in real time, introduces a level of intelligence, scalability, and accuracy never seen before. Imagine the same inventory management task we discussed earlier. Instead of manual cross-checking and data entry, an AI system can continuously monitor stock levels in real time, autonomously trigger reorders when the stock reaches a predefined level, and even optimize the reordering quantity based on forecasted demand.

AI isn't just automating tasks; it's performing them at a speed and precision that far outstrips human capability. Customer service, data analysis, invoice processing, inventory management—the scope of tasks AI can automate is vast and continuously expanding.

But the impact of AI on business process automation isn't limited to task execution. It extends into decision-making, providing valuable insights businesses can leverage to make more informed decisions. For instance, an AI system can aggregate and analyze data from many sources—sales data, customer feedback, market trends, and even social media sentiment—and distill it into actionable insights. Imagine having real-time reports on market performance, predictive analysis of sales trends, or granular insights into customer behavior patterns. That's the power of AI.

Furthermore, AI's capability to learn and adapt over time means that these systems continuously improve, becoming more efficient and accurate as they handle more data and tasks. This continuous learning feature of AI models ensures they evolve with the business, adapting to changes and catering to emerging needs.

Introducing AI into business process automation signifies the dawn of a new era. It represents a fundamental shift away from the manual, error-prone processes of the past towards a future where tasks are performed with speed, precision, and intelligence. This future is here, and it's time for businesses to embrace it.

In summary, integrating AI in business process automation revolutionizes efficiency, speed, and accuracy, allowing businesses to scale without proportionally increasing costs. By analyzing complex data, AI supports informed decision-making and real-time monitoring, leading to cost savings and continuous improvement. It enhances customer experiences through personalization and strengthens risk management. Employees are freed from mundane tasks, focusing on meaningful work that boosts satisfaction and engagement. In a competitive landscape, AI is not just an enhancement; it's a strategic imperative that drives innovation, growth, and value delivery.

Real-Life Example - Walmart: Revolutionizing Retail with AI

Imagine walking into a Walmart store and finding everything you need right where you expect it to be. The shelves are always stocked, and you receive personalized recommendations that seem to read your mind. Behind this seamless shopping experience is an invisible force—Walmart's AI technology.

Walmart, one of the largest retailers globally, has harnessed the power of AI to enhance its operations, improve customer experience, and stay ahead in a fiercely competitive market. From inventory management to customer service, AI has permeated every aspect of Walmart's business processes.

Walmart's AI algorithms manage its inventory with remarkable efficiency. By analyzing data and forecasting demand, the AI ensures that shelves are always adequately stocked, reducing instances of out-of-stock items and improving customer satisfaction. This AI-powered inventory management is a game-changer, transforming how Walmart operates its vast retail network.

But the magic of AI doesn't stop at inventory management. Walmart uses AI to offer personalized recommendations to its customers, both online and in-store. By analyzing customer browsing patterns, purchase history, and demographic data, AI algorithms suggest relevant products and promotions tailored to individual preferences. This level of personalization enhances the customer's shopping experience and increases the likelihood of purchasing.

Walmart's AI journey extends to customer service as well. The company has integrated AI chatbots and virtual assistants into its customer service channels. These intelligent systems can handle customer inquiries, provide product information, and assist with common issues, such as order tracking and returns. This AI-powered customer service reduces waiting times, provides 24/7 support, and ensures consistent service quality across multiple touchpoints.

The benefits of AI for Walmart are manifold. By automating various processes and optimizing operations, AI helps Walmart streamline its business, improving efficiency and cost savings. For example, AI algorithms can optimize transportation routes, reduce fuel consumption, and minimize delivery delays. AI-powered systems can also identify inefficiencies in supply chain management and suggest optimization strategies, reducing waste and minimizing costs.

Moreover, AI enables Walmart to provide personalized shopping experiences tailored to customers' individual preferences and needs. This level of personalization enhances customer satisfaction, fosters loyalty, and increases the likelihood of repeat purchases.

In essence, Walmart's adoption of AI is a testament to the transformative power of this technology in the retail sector. It showcases how AI can revolutionize business processes, enhance customer experience, and provide a competitive edge in today's digital age. Walmart's AI journey is a shining example of how businesses can harness AI to drive innovation, efficiency, and growth.

AI Integration Across Business Process Automation Areas

AI can be integrated across various areas of business process automation, each with its unique benefits and transformative potential. As we have seen in use cases mentioned earlier, here are some key areas where artificial intelligence can be effectively applied:

- **Sales and Marketing Automation**: AI can automate various aspects of sales and marketing, from lead generation to customer segmentation, personalized marketing, and sales forecasting. AI-powered CRM systems can automate follow-ups, track customer interactions, and provide insights into customer needs. This can lead to hyper-targeted marketing campaigns, improved sales conversion rates, and enhanced customer relationships.

- **Supply Chain and Inventory Management**: AI can automate and optimize various aspects of supply chain management, from demand forecasting to manufacturing, inventory management, logistics, and supplier relationship management. AI can predict demand based on historical data and market trends, optimize inventory levels to prevent overstocking or stockouts, automate reordering processes, and expect potential supply chain disruptions.

- **Customer Service**: AI-powered chatbots and virtual assistants can automate customer service, handling routine queries, providing instant responses, and freeing human agents to address more complex issues. AI can also analyze customer feedback and behavior to provide insights into customer satisfaction and identify areas for improvement.

- **Finance and Accounting**: AI can automate various financial processes, from invoice processing and expense management to financial reporting and forecasting. AI can reduce errors, speed up processing times, and provide real-time insights into financial performance.
- **Human Resources**: AI can automate various HR processes, from recruitment and onboarding to performance management and employee engagement. AI can screen resumes, schedule interviews, provide personalized onboarding experiences, track employee performance, and predict employee turnover.
- **IT Operations:** AI can automate various IT processes, from system monitoring and incident management to cybersecurity and data management. AI can predict and prevent system failures, detect and respond to security threats, and optimize data storage and processing.

Integrating AI across these areas allows businesses to automate routine tasks, improve efficiency and accuracy, gain valuable insights, and free up human resources for more strategic initiatives. This can lead to significant cost savings, improved operational efficiency, and enhanced competitiveness in the market.

AI-Powered Business Process Automation

Stage Name	Stage Description	What Happens	How AI Can Help	Example AI Tools
Discovery	Understanding the processes	Identify repetitive, rule-based processes across the organization	AI can analyze workflow patterns to identify processes that can be automated	Celonis, IBM Automation
Modeling	Defining the process workflow	Develop a clear, standardized workflow for the process	AI can help in modeling the workflows, identifying possible improvements or redundancies	IBM Blueworks, AISERA, Levity

Automation	Implementing the process	Apply AI tools to automate the identified processes	AI can automate repetitive tasks, reducing human effort and errors	UiPath, Zapier, Automation Anywhere
Monitoring	Oversight of the process	Monitor the automated processes to ensure they're functioning correctly	AI can continuously monitor the processes, provide real-time insights and identify any issues	New Relic, Dynatrace
Optimization	Improving the process	Identify areas of further improvement in the automated processes	AI can analyze process data to find inefficiencies and suggest optimizations	Kissflow, Appian

Live Case Study:
AI in Business Process Automation

Figure 30 - Streamlining Call Center Operations and Hotel Onboarding with AI at Voyager Inc. (Source – Midjourney)

Context: Karen, the manager of a small call center for a thriving travel company, Voyager Inc., was tasked with finding and onboarding new hotels to the company's platform. Her responsibilities were vast and complex, involving reaching out to potential hotels, vetting them for quality, closing contracts, and onboarding them. Recognizing the potential of AI in business operations, Karen decided to transform her call center with the help of AI tools. Let's look at her journey.

⚒ AI tools used:

- ChatGPT (For creating custom emails, responding to hotel queries, contract drafts, etc.)
- Webautomation (For scraping the hotel leads list)
- SignalHire (For getting the contact details of shortlisted leads)
- Crystal Knows (For decoding the lead personality)
- Zapier (For automating lead comm funnel, contract signup, onboarding and engagement)
- Calendly (For scheduling appointments on autopilot)
- Slack (For customer support while onboarding)
- Oneflow (For automated contract management)

💡 Step-by-Step Playbook

Step 1: Automating Lead Generation

Karen began by automating her lead generation process. She used web scraping sites like **WebAutomation** to continuously scrape hotels information from Google, TripAdvisor and Booking.com. Using **Zapier**, an automation tool, she transferred the scraped or submitted leads information to a Google Sheet.

Below is a sample of scraped data from London, which is then transferred to the master google sheet, which she has connected to Zapier to process the next steps in automation as soon as a new row is added.

Domain	Title	Score	# of Reviews	Review	Price	Currency	* Rating	# if Rooms
booking.com	Lovely 2-Bedroom Victorian Flats	7.8	50 reviews	Good	['Å£168']	GBP	3	35
booking.com	CENTRAL APARTMENT PADDINGTON	7.5	73 reviews	Good	['Å£350']	GBP	4	35
booking.com	Affordable Rooms in shared flat, London Bridge	7	73 reviews	Good	['Å£119']	GBP	5	40
booking.com	Holland Road Stays	5.2	190 reviews	Good	['Å£110']	GBP	4	60
booking.com	Rest Boutique Notting Hill	8.6	90 reviews	Fabulous	['Å£132']	GBP	5	80
booking.com	Ember Locke	9.1	24 reviews	Superb	['Å£179']	GBP	4	100
booking.com	Great Scotland Yard Hotel, part of Hyatt	8.7	823 reviews	Fabulous	['Å£383']	GBP	4	120
booking.com	Bermondsey Square Hotel - A Bespoke Hotel	7.9	2,338 reviews	Good	['Å£179']	GBP	2	30
booking.com	Draycott Hotel by Iconic Luxury Hotels	8.5	366 reviews	Very good	['Å£335']	GBP	3	45
booking.com	Princes Square	7	168 reviews	Good	['Å£140']	GBP	4	45

Figure 31 - Leads scraped via Webautomation Tool

Step 2: Lead Qualification

Karen then used automation within **Zapier** to qualify the leads-based criteria like # of Reviews > 100, Room Price > 100 GBP, Number of Rooms > 30, Star Rating > 3. These qualified leads are then transferred to a filtered and cleaned-up leads list in a Google sheet document, which Karen used for personal multi-channel outreach.

Step 3: Fetching Lead Contact

Taking the example of Great Scotland Yard Hotel from Step 1, Karen searched the relevant profiles of decision makers for the Hotel on Linkedin and then used tools like **SignalHire** to fetch the lead contact details.

Step 4: Lead Profiling

Karen then used Tool **Crystal Knows** to understand the lead personality to craft personalized and compelling communication accordingly.

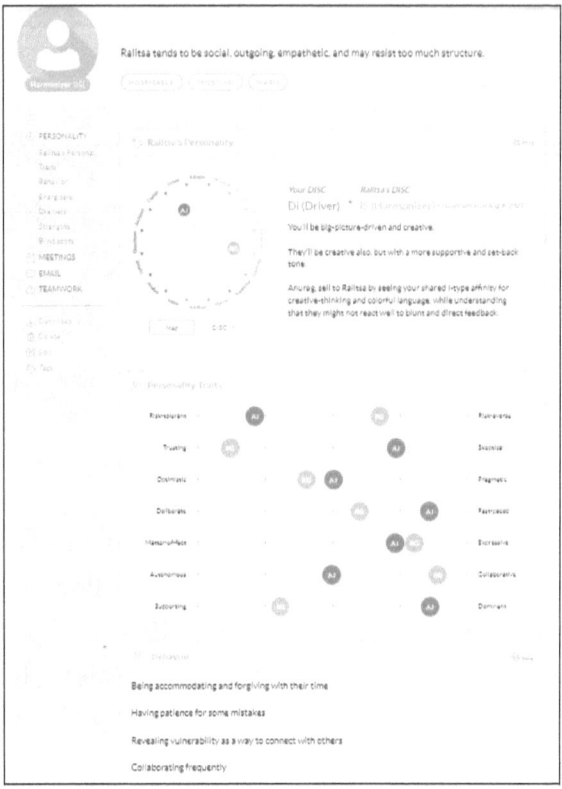

Figure 32 - Lead Profiling with Crystal Knows

Step 5: Drafting Initial Contact Emails

With the help of AI tools like **ChatGPT**, Karen drafted an initial contact email that was friendly and persuasive, and the tonality was in line with the lead personality. She set up an automated process through Zapier that used this email template to send personalized emails to the contact and a **Calendly** link to automate appointments. Customizing emails based on the recipient's personality helped Karen achieve 10x conversion for her emails.

Step 6: Automating Follow-ups

Karen used AI to automate her follow-ups as well, in case the person did not respond to the initial mail. She set up a Zap in **Zapier** that triggered a follow-up email funnel if she didn't receive a reply within a specified time frame to ensure that no potential lead was missed due to a lack of follow-up.

If the lead responded positively, Karen got on a quick call basis the appointment booked by the lead via Calendly and then moved the converted information to an automated contract process.

Step 7: Streamlining Contract Creation

Karen used **ChatGPT** to draft the initial contract based on standard terms and conditions for contract negotiations. She streamlined the negotiation process using AI to prepare responses to common negotiation points, after which she initiated an automated contract creation process via **Oneflow**.

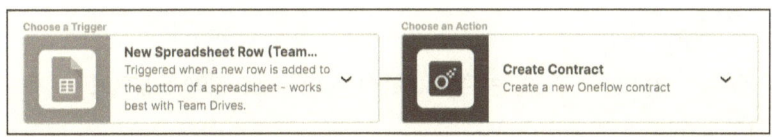

Figure 33 - Sample Zapier Automation To Trigger Contract When Lead is Converted

Step 8: Automating Onboarding

The onboarding process began after a hotel signed the partnership agreement with Voyager Inc. Karen used Slack, integrated with

Zapier, to automatically create a new onboarding channel for each hotel. She also trained **ChatGPT** on the entire process. All questions from the partner were routed to ChatGPT based on the Zapier Automation below, with ChatGPT responding as a virtual assistant, setting the entire end-to-end onboarding process on auto-pilot.

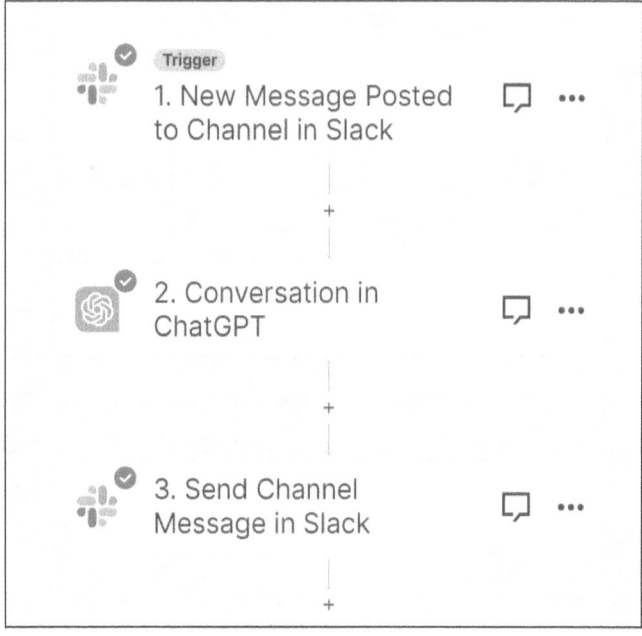

Figure 34 - Zapier Automation for Onboarding Support

Step 9: Managing Relationships and Regular Follow-ups

Finally, Karen leveraged AI to maintain relationships with the onboarded hotels. She used AI tools to schedule regular check-ins, send satisfaction surveys, and receive feedback. In case of any issues or concerns raised by the hotels, Karen set up automated alerts that notified the relevant team members to address them promptly. This helped Karen scale her operations by 10x with the help of AI in her business.

Conclusion

By integrating AI tools into her operations, Karen increased her call center's efficiency significantly, allowing her team to onboard more hotels faster and maintain excellent relationships with them. Karen's story serves as an inspiration for other businesses looking to harness the power of AI to streamline their operations. Her strategic use of AI in automating lead generation, initial contact, follow-ups, contract creation, onboarding, and relationship management demonstrates the transformative potential of AI in business process automation.

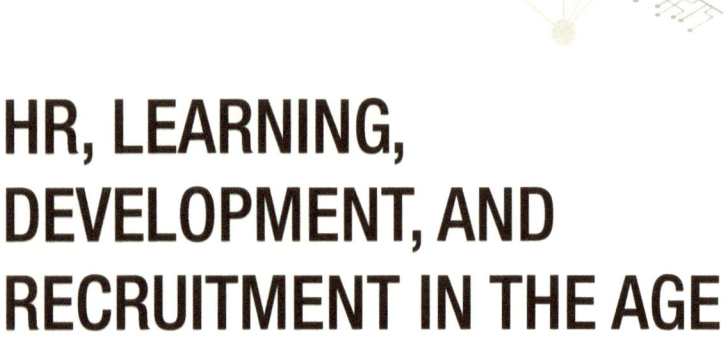

HR, LEARNING, DEVELOPMENT, AND RECRUITMENT IN THE AGE OF AI

> *"Hire character. Train skill."*
> *– Peter Schutz*

Reflecting on my leadership journey, I recall the massive task of scaling my team from a humble few to hundreds of talented people. The process was exhaustive, from sifting through thousands of resumes to selecting the best fits and onboarding and upskilling each new member of our rapidly growing organization.

As the leader of this venture, the sheer magnitude of the recruitment process felt like navigating uncharted waters. The method of reviewing resumes was like sieving through sand for nuggets of gold, an effort that absorbed significant time and energy. The hours dedicated to conducting interviews and pinpointing the ideal candidates were steep, starkly contrasting the lean, agile startup environment I had been accustomed to.

The mountainous task of onboarding was equally daunting. Every recruit represented a considerable investment of time from the existing team, as we worked tirelessly to familiarize them with the company's processes, ethos, and values. The entire process felt akin to running an uphill marathon when coupled with the constant need for upskilling.

Then came the critical role of ensuring continuous growth and development. This process involved understanding individual needs, crafting personalized learning experiences, and fostering an environment conducive to professional growth. The team's engagement and morale were pivotal in the process, necessitating regular surveys and feedback mechanisms to gauge sentiment and address concerns.

From recruitment to retention, the entire journey felt like a manually intensive roller coaster for my HR team. As a business owner, a thought frequently crossed my mind: Was there a way to expedite these processes? Could we leverage technology to make them more efficient, perhaps 10x faster? Well, AI presents a promising solution to this age-old question.

As we delve deeper into this chapter, we will explore how AI can revolutionize the HR, learning, development, and recruitment landscapes. Imagine an AI-assisted recruitment process where machine learning algorithms sift through resumes to find the best fit. In this system, onboarding and upskilling become streamlined, personalized experiences.

Envision a future where performance management becomes autonomous and engagement surveys become real-time and highly interactive. AI helps us understand our team's morale and proposes actionable insights. Imagine how much more time could be spent growing the business, identifying new opportunities, and building solid partnerships.

The future of HR, learning, development, and recruitment lies in embracing AI. And this chapter aims to illuminate the pathway towards that future. As we journey ahead, let's delve into this exciting potential and how AI can transform these critical business aspects.

The Conventional Way

Human touchpoints dominate every stage in the traditional landscape of human resources, learning, development, and recruitment. Hiring managers face the arduous task of poring over countless resumes, each demanding scrutiny. The interviewing process is even more challenging, involving coordinating with multiple stakeholders, rigorous scheduling, and personal engagement.

It's a process often guided more by intuition than data, a subjective journey through human judgment. Learning and development, too, are shackled by one-size-fits-all paradigms, with success hinging on an individual's pace and learning style rather than tailored, responsive strategies. Feedback mechanisms are often sporadic and subjective, relying on surveys and annual reviews rather than continuous, data-driven insights.

The conventional method has several drawbacks:

Time-Consuming: Manual sorting of resumes, conducting interviews, and making hiring decisions is a labor-intensive process that can take weeks or even months. Similarly, designing and implementing training programs requires a significant investment of time.

Lack of Personalization: Traditional learning and development programs may not cater to individual learning styles or needs, leading to potential gaps in skill development.

Inefficiency: The inability to quickly process large volumes of data (e.g., resumes or employee feedback) can lead to missed opportunities and inefficiencies in the HR process.

Bias: Unconscious biases can creep into the recruitment and evaluation process, potentially leading to unfair outcomes.

Limited Accessibility: Traditional HR services, including support and training, are typically confined to office hours and specific locations, limiting accessibility for remote or non-traditional employees.

While rich in human engagement, this entire process is fraught with inefficiencies and inconsistencies, crying out for a transformation towards more streamlined, personalized, and data-driven methodologies.

Enter Artificial Intelligence

Artificial intelligence has the potential to revolutionize the way HR functions are conducted, addressing many of the shortcomings of traditional methods:

Efficiency and Speed: AI can quickly process large volumes of data, significantly reducing the time required for recruitment and other HR functions. Machine learning algorithms can sift through thousands of resumes in a fraction of the time it would take a human to identify suitable candidates for further assessment.

Personalization: AI can personalize learning and development programs, catering to individual learning styles and needs. This results in more effective training and better skill development.

Bias Reduction: AI can help reduce unconscious biases in recruitment by focusing on objective measures such as skills and experience, leading to more fair and diverse hiring practices.

Increased Accessibility: AI can provide HR services round the clock, improving accessibility for all employees regardless of location or working hours.

Predictive Analysis: AI can use data to predict trends and outcomes, such as employee turnover or the success of recruitment campaigns, which can help organizations to be proactive rather than reactive in their HR strategies.

Real-Life Example:
IBM: Leveraging AI to Humanize HR and Boost Efficiency

Picture a world where HR tasks are no longer a maze of administrative work but a streamlined process that allows for more nuanced, human touch points. This is not a distant future but a present reality at IBM. This global technology giant has harnessed the power of artificial intelligence (AI) to revolutionize its HR operations.

IBM's journey with AI began over a decade ago with Watson, its AI computing system. Today, the company has developed a suite of AI tools designed to help businesses run more efficiently and accurately while maximizing productivity. One of these tools is AskHR, a virtual assistant that provides employees with instant answers to their HR-related queries, from vacation policy to training requirements. Instead of sifting through portals or waiting for responses from HR, employees can ask Watson, which uses data based on their tenure, location, and days already used.

Another innovative application of AI at IBM is in performance evaluation. IBM's AI platform determines which employees qualify for a raise or promotion. It sifts through data, including past performance ratings, skills, training records, and length of employment, and then sends recommendations to managers for review. This automation saves time and allows managers to focus on coaching employees on how they can improve and progress in their careers.

The impact of this AI-driven automation is significant. IBM's HR department has saved close to 12,000 hours in the last 18 months by automating systems that previously required back-and-forth exchanges between managers and employees.

"We've got over 280 different AI automations running inside HR right now; it's making HR more human because we're spending time on things that matter," says Nickle LaMoreaux, IBM's Chief Human Resources Officer. ""

IBM's journey with AI in HR is a shining example for businesses worldwide. It showcases how AI can revolutionize HR operations, enhance employee experience, and provide a competitive edge in today's digital age.

Artificial Intelligence Integration in HR Function

The AI-powered HR Transformation Matrix is a comprehensive framework that outlines how AI can be integrated across various HR functions. This matrix is a roadmap for organizations leveraging AI in their HR processes.

- **Recruitment**: AI can automate the screening of resumes, identifying candidates with the right skills and experience. AI can also schedule interviews, conduct initial screening interviews using chatbots, and predict the likelihood of a candidate's success in a role.
- **Onboarding**: AI can personalize onboarding, providing new hires with tailored information and resources. AI can also monitor the onboarding process, identifying issues or bottlenecks and suggesting improvements.
- **Learning and Development**: AI can personalize learning and development programs, recommending courses based on an employee's current skills and career goals. AI can also track progress and provide feedback, helping employees to improve and grow.
- **Performance Management**: AI can automate the collection and analysis of performance data, providing managers with real-time insights into their team's performance. AI can also predict future performance based on historical data, helping managers to identify potential issues and opportunities.

- **Employee Engagement**: AI can analyze employee feedback and sentiment, providing real-time insights into employee engagement. AI can also suggest actions to improve concentration, such as changes to the work environment or management practices.
- **Payroll and Benefits Administration**: AI can automate payroll processing, ensuring accuracy and compliance with tax and labor laws. AI can also manage benefits administration, personalizing benefits packages based on employee preferences and needs and automating enrollment and changes to benefits.
- **Workforce Planning and Analytics**: AI can analyze workforce data to identify trends and patterns, helping HR leaders make data-driven decisions about hiring, retention, and workforce development. AI can also predict future workforce needs based on business growth, employee turnover, and market trends.
- **Talent Management**: AI can help identify high-potential employees, predict future leaders, and suggest personalized career development plans. AI can also support succession planning by identifying skills gaps and presenting internal candidates for critical roles.

By integrating AI across these areas, organizations can streamline their HR processes, improve efficiency and accuracy, and provide a better experience for their employees. The future of HR is here, and AI powers it.

AI-Powered Human Resource Management

Stage Name	Stage Description	What Happens	How AI Can Help	Example AI Tools
Recruitment	Sourcing and screening candidates	Potential candidates for a job role are identified, screened, and shortlisted.	AI can automate job postings, CV screening, and shortlisting of candidates based on job requirements	LinkedIn Talent Solutions, Eightfold.ai
Interviewing	Conducting interviews	Candidates are interviewed to assess their suitability	AI can facilitate video interviews, analyze candidate responses and non-verbal cues	HireVue, MyInterview
Onboarding	Introducing new hires to the organization	New hires are oriented to their roles, responsibilities, and organizational culture	AI can automate the onboarding process, making it faster and more consistent.	Talmundo, Click Boarding

Learning and Development	Building employee skills	Employees are trained for their roles, and their skills are developed	AI can provide personalized learning paths and measure learning outcomes	Docebo, EdCast
Performance Management	Evaluating employee performance	Employee performance is assessed, and feedback is given	AI can provide real-time performance analytics and help in setting fair, data-driven goals	Betterworks, Reflektive
Employee Engagement	Ensuring employee satisfaction	Engagement activities are conducted to maintain a positive work environment.	AI can analyze employee sentiment and suggest personalized engagement activities.	Glint, Peakon
Retention	Maintaining a stable workforce	Strategies are implemented to reduce employee turnover	AI can help with workforce planning, compensation and more	Visier, Workday
Offboarding	Managing the exit process	Employees leaving the organization are managed	AI can ensure smooth offboarding and knowledge transfer	SAP SuccessFactors, BambooHR

Live Case Study:
Streamlining HR Operations with AI

Figure 35 - SparkLabs Office Image generated by AI (Source: Midjourney)

John, an HR professional at a fast-growing tech startup, Sparklabs, juggled various responsibilities. From recruitment to onboarding, employee engagement to growth and development, John was the sole HR force in the company. However, the manual nature of these tasks was becoming increasingly challenging. Recognizing the potential of AI, John decided to transform his HR operations. Let's walk through John's journey.

⚒ AI tools used:

- ChatGPT (For interview content, onboarding playbook, and growth coaching)
- Botpress (For automated onboarding and support)
- Zappyhire/Vervoe (For automating the entire recruitment process)
- Microsoft Office (Forms and Excel for data management and visual analysis)
- Zapier (For workflow automation)
- Brevo (For email automation)

💡 Step-by-Step Playbook

Step 1: Crafting Job Descriptions

John began by revamping the job descriptions. He used **ChatGPT**, an AI-powered writing tool, to create comprehensive, inclusive, and attractive job postings. The AI tool suggested changes that made his job descriptions more appealing to a broader talent pool.

Step 2: Automating Resume Screening

With hundreds of applications pouring in, screening resumes was a daunting task. John turned to **Google Sheets** and **Zapier** to automate this process. He created a system where the applicants' information was automatically transferred to a Google Sheet. Using Zapier, he transferred the candidate info to ChatGPT, trained on the job requirements, and **ChatGPT** auto-screened and shortlisted candidates based on job requirements, drastically reducing the time spent on resume screening.

Scoring Jordan Smith's Resume Based on JD:

Criteria	Score (out of 10)
Years of Experience in Product Management	8
Experience with Agile Methodologies	10
Proven track record of launching products	10
Familiarity with Tech Industry	9
Analytical and Problem-solving skills	9
Communication abilities	9
Proficiency in Product Management tools	10
Customer-centric mindset	9
Collaborative and Team-oriented	10
Passionate about innovation	9

Total Score: 93 out of 100

Strengths and Opportunities for Jordan Smith:

Strengths	Opportunities
Solid experience in product management.	Expand more into emerging tech trends.
Proven track record of successful product launches.	Enhance global market understanding.
Familiar with agile methodologies.	Improve foreign language proficiency.
Strong communication and collaboration skills.	Engage in more end-user research.
Proficient in product management tools.	Seek feedback more proactively.

Figure 36 - Sample Scoring Of Candidate Done by CHATGPT

Over time, John also deployed AI tools like **Zappyhire** and **Vervoe** to automate the recruitment workflow completely. See the sample screenshot below:

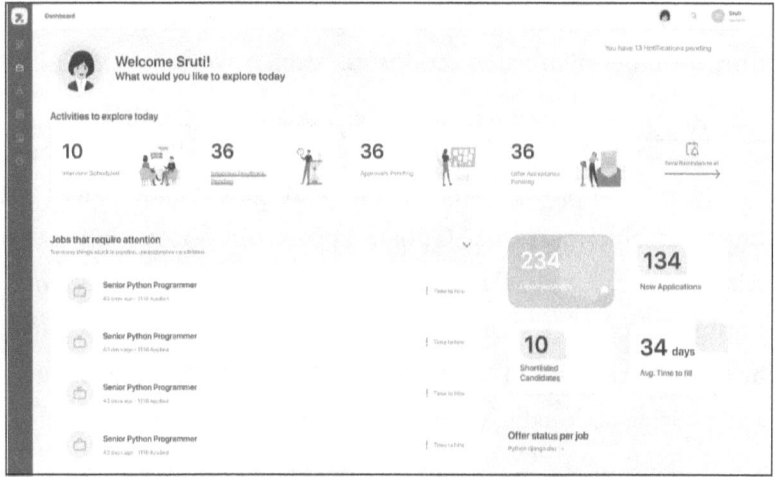

Figure 37 - Zappyhire AI Tool Recruiter Dashboard

Step 3: Streamlining Interviews

John used **ChatGPT** to create a questionnaire to interview the shortlisted candidates. The candidates' responses were recorded and analyzed using an AI tool like **Yoodli**, focusing on their words and expressions to gauge their fit for the role.

Step 4: Automating Onboarding

Upon successful selection, the new hires were onboarded. John used **Brevo** and Zapier to streamline and automate the onboarding process. The new hires received necessary information and checklists through an automated email funnel, ensuring the onboarding process was smooth and efficient.

Step 5: Upskilling for the Role

John trained **Botpress** on all the company documents, processes, tools, and systems, which then served as a go-to resource for the new hires if they had any questions. This helped John free up time for more high-value actions vs. reactive work.

Step 6: Conducting Engagement Surveys and Analysis

To gauge employee satisfaction and understand areas of improvement, John used Google Forms and Sheets, integrated with Zapier. ChatGPT created engagement surveys, Google Forms collected responses and transferred entries to Google Sheets, which then used the AI capabilities to analyze the data and provide actionable insights.

Step 7: Personalizing Growth and Development Plans

Finally, to ensure the growth of the employees, John used **ChatGPT** for personalized training programs. He created a system where the AI tool recommended courses based on each employee's role, skills, and career aspirations.

John's strategic implementation of AI tools transformed his HR operations, making them more efficient and effective. His story inspires other HR professionals in small and expanding firms, highlighting how AI can streamline HR processes and drive growth. His use of simple yet powerful tools like Google Sheets, Botpress, Zapier, and ChatGPT demonstrates the transformative potential of AI in HR operations.

GOING DIGITAL: AI AND YOUR WEB, APP, SOCIAL MEDIA STRATEGY

> *"We don't have a choice on whether we do social media; the question is how well we do it."*
> *– Erik Qualman*

Reflecting on my leadership journey, I recall a pivotal moment when we decided to take our traditionally strong brands into the digital realm. It aimed to better connect with our modern consumers, who were increasingly present and active in digital spaces. The shift involved reimagining everything – from creating an engaging brand-aligned app to developing a high-conversion website and telling compelling brand stories that hooked our customers.

But venturing into this digital expanse was challenging. One of our primary concerns was discovery: How could we ensure our meticulously crafted content, shiny new website, and user-friendly app were preserved in the sea of digital content? How could we enhance visibility without a hefty marketing budget? These questions led us to delve into search engine optimization and explore ways to improve our content's discoverability.

The quest to maximize return on investment from our online marketing spend was another challenge. We had an ambitious ROAS target and realized this required a strategic blend of impactful content, clever advertising, and continuous engagement with our audience.

Our presence on social media added another layer of complexity. We needed content that didn't just blend into the digital landscape but stood out and caught the eye. Increasing follower engagement and growing our page was a task that required creativity, resourcefulness, and a deep understanding of our audience.

We needed to ensure a consistent and engaging user experience across all platforms as we extended our brand touchpoints into the digital sphere. This entailed maintaining our brand's promise at each touchpoint, whether on our app, website, or social media pages.

Data was a crucial aspect of this digital journey. With a wealth of customer feedback and online chatter about our brand, we faced the challenge of accessing and analyzing this data. We needed to comprehend our brand's online perception, identify the positives, and address the areas of concern.

Navigating these challenges, we managed to grow our online brands significantly. However, the journey involved extensive trial and error, experimentation, and a considerable investment of time and resources. Looking back now, AI could have been our compass, guiding us to streamline our processes, enhancing efficiency, and potentially achieving 10x results.

In this chapter, we'll explore how AI can power your digital journey, from creating your website to improving content discoverability, optimizing return on marketing investments, managing social media, and enhancing user experience. AI holds the potential to truly transform every aspect of going digital, and we're about to embark on a fascinating exploration of these possibilities.

The Conventional Way

In the past, establishing a digital presence was a fairly linear process. A company would set up a website, create profiles on social media platforms, and develop an app. Marketing teams were responsible for crafting content to populate these platforms and engage customers. Search Engine Optimization (SEO) was manually done by incorporating relevant keywords into the website content and meta descriptions.

Expanding upon the conventional way of managing a company's digital presence, you can think of it as attempting to sail a vast sea with only a rudimentary compass and map. Every move was based on assumptions and existing practices rather than concrete data or automated solutions.

Setting up the online infrastructure—the website, social media platforms, and potentially an app—was akin to building the ship itself. The design, the interfaces, and the overall user experience were all meticulously crafted, aiming to make the voyage as smooth as possible for the customer.

Yet, without real-time feedback or advanced analytical tools, it was challenging to validate whether these designs were effective or genuinely resonated with the user base.

In the world of content creation, marketing teams were like the sailors navigating this digital ship. With every piece of content—a blog post, a social media update, or an app notification—they cast lines out into the sea of potential customers, hoping for a bite. The process was labor-intensive and relied heavily on creativity, intuition, and sometimes sheer luck.

Then came the challenge of SEO. It was the lighthouse that could make your business visible amidst the fog of online content. Keywords were carefully sewn into the fabric of the website, aiming to attract the attention of search engine algorithms. It was a process that required constant vigilance and fine-tuning as the algorithms and trends evolved.

Social media platforms were an entirely different beast to tackle. Here, engagement often boiled down to a volume game. The more content you could churn out, the higher the chance of gaining visibility. But this was not a precise science. It was predicting what content would stick or go viral too much work. It was like throwing many messages in bottles into the ocean and hoping someone would find and open them.

And when it came to calculating ROI, businesses often found themselves squinting at blurred lines. Tracking which marketing strategies drove the most traffic or which platform yielded the highest conversions required manual data crunching and analysis.

User experience was another territory often left uncharted. While businesses had an idea of how their website or app should be navigated, there needed to be a way to understand how users interacted with these platforms. Most user experience enhancements were reactive, based on user feedback, rather than proactive, leading to a game of catch-up rather than innovation.

The journey was still being determined as businesses sailed these vast, unpredictable digital seas. While they often managed to stay afloat and progress, there was always a nagging question: Is there a better way?

Enter Artificial Intelligence

AI fundamentally changes how businesses approach their digital strategies. It offers tools and techniques to automate routine tasks, derive insights from data, and provide personalized experiences.

Expanding on how AI revolutionizes the digital strategy landscape, it can be likened to providing businesses with a sophisticated navigation system, complete with radar and autopilot, for their digital voyage.

Automation of routine tasks is one of AI's most prominent features. It's like having a tireless crew that can handle tasks such as sending marketing emails, updating social media posts, and responding to common customer inquiries. Automation reduces the manual workload, ensures round-the-clock service, and provides a consistent user experience.

Regarding SEO, AI transforms it from guesswork to a strategic exercise. AI algorithms can analyze web traffic and user behavior, identify trends, and suggest optimal keywords to boost visibility. It's akin to having an intelligent lighthouse that adapts its beam according to the current visibility conditions and the position of your ship, ensuring you are always visible to your target audience.

The content creation and marketing field also undergoes a significant transformation with AI. Machine learning algorithms can analyze customer data to understand preferences, behaviors, and engagement patterns. This empowers businesses to create and deliver more targeted and impactful content. It's as if your messages in bottles are now GPS-enabled, reaching the right audience at the right time.

AI's power in sentiment analysis transforms how businesses understand their social media presence. AI can gauge public sentiment about your brand, products, or services by analyzing comments, reviews, and conversations. This valuable insight can guide your social media strategy, product development, and customer service. It's like having a dedicated scout on every social media platform, continuously reporting back with updates.

In customer service, AI can be leveraged to deploy chatbots that can handle routine inquiries, freeing up your human resources to deal with more complex issues. Picture a robot on your ship that's always available to assist customers with their queries or issues, no matter the time.

The ability of AI to track, analyze, and derive insights from your marketing efforts is invaluable. It can shed light on the effectiveness of your campaigns, identify trends, and predict future outcomes.

This makes marketing more strategic and outcome-oriented. It's like having an intelligent dashboard on your ship that shows your current position, forecasts the weather, and suggests the best course.

Lastly, AI's ability to personalize the user experience can make all the difference in your digital strategy. AI can predict user needs, recommend products, and customize content by analyzing user behavior. It's like having a personal concierge for each customer, making them feel valued and enhancing their engagement with your brand.

In a nutshell, Integrating AI into your digital strategy is like equipping your ship with state-of-the-art navigation tools, enabling you to confidently and precisely chart the vast digital ocean. AI automates routine tasks, allowing your team to focus on strategic initiatives. It enhances SEO, boosts online visibility, and personalizes content creation based on customer preferences, improving engagement and conversion rates.

Real-Life Examples:
Expedia: Soaring High with AI

When planning a vacation, the sheer volume of options can be overwhelming. But imagine a platform that understands your preferences, streamlines your choices, and offers personalized recommendations. This isn't a future vision; it's the present-day reality at Expedia.

Expedia, a titan in the online travel industry, is pioneering a new era of travel planning powered by Artificial Intelligence (AI). With a vast network spanning over 168 million loyalty members and more than 50,000 business partners, Expedia's treasure trove of data—amounting to an impressive 70 petabytes—is its compass. Stored on the AWS cloud, this data is the foundation upon which Expedia is building its AI-driven future.

By integrating ChatGPT into their app, Expedia has transformed how travelers plan their journeys. Instead of sifting through countless options, users can now have an intuitive "chat" with the app, discussing travel plans as if conversing with a seasoned travel advisor. This AI-driven conversation offers personalized travel suggestions, from accommodations to activities, all tailored to the user's preferences.

Beyond chat, Expedia's AI algorithms are complex behind the scenes. They manage inventory, ensuring the most relevant travel options are always at the forefront. By analyzing customer behaviors, these algorithms also curate personalized travel recommendations, enhancing the user experience and increasing the likelihood of bookings.

Customer service, too, has been elevated with AI. Expedia's integration of AI chatbots ensures that travelers receive timely, consistent support, whether they're inquiring about a booking or seeking travel advice.

In essence, Expedia's embrace of AI is reshaping the travel industry. Seamlessly integrating advanced technologies, they're enhancing the traveler's experience and setting a new standard for the digital travel marketplace. As Expedia charts its AI-driven course, it stands as a beacon for other businesses, showcasing the transformative power of AI in the digital age.

AI-Enhanced Digital Transformation Matrix

Let's look at how AI can be applied across the digital spectrum for your business:

- **Web**: AI can optimize your website's SEO, personalize content for each visitor, analyze user behavior to improve the user experience, and even create websites in a single click. AI-powered tools can generate fully functional websites based on user preferences, significantly reducing the time and effort required in website development.
- **App**: AI can personalize the app experience, recommend products or services, analyze user behavior to improve app design and functionality, and even help create prototypes and fully functional apps with no code. Platforms like Bubble leverage AI to enable users to build sophisticated apps without coding knowledge, making app development more accessible.
- **Social Media**: AI can analyze social media sentiment, automate post scheduling, personalize content to increase engagement, and generate complete social media content, including text, speech, and video. AI-powered tools can create engaging and relevant content, reducing the burden on your content creation team and ensuring a consistent posting schedule.
- **Content Creation**: AI can analyze customer preferences and behavior to create targeted and impactful content. AI can generate content, including blog posts, articles, and social media updates, freeing your team to focus on strategic tasks.
- **Marketing**: AI can track and analyze marketing efforts, predict future trends, and optimize ad targeting to improve ROI. AI can also automate marketing campaigns, from email

marketing to social media advertising, ensuring consistent and timely communication with your audience.

- **Customer Service**: AI can automate routine customer inquiries, analyze customer feedback, and predict customer needs to improve service quality. AI-powered chatbots can provide 24/7 customer service, handling common questions and freeing your team to focus on more complex issues.

By integrating AI across these areas, organizations can streamline their digital strategies, improve efficiency and accuracy, and provide a better customer experience. The future of digital design is here, and AI powers it.

AI-Powered Online Business

Stage Name	Stage Description	What Happens	How AI Can Help	Example AI Tools
Web Development	Creating and maintaining websites	Websites are developed, updated, and optimized	AI can automate coding, improve website accessibility, and provide intelligent recommendations.	Wix ADI, Framer
App Development	Creating and maintaining applications	Mobile and desktop applications are developed and updated	AI can automate app testing, enhance user experience with personalized features	Bubble, Uizard, Kissflow
Content Generation	Producing engaging content	Content for web, app, and social media platforms is generated	AI can create content, curate personalized content, and optimize content strategy	Jasper, Wordhero, Clickup

SEO	Optimizing visibility on search engines	Website and content is optimized for search engine visibility	AI can predict SEO trends, optimize content for SEO, and provide insights for better ranking	SEO.ai, BrightEdge, Market Brew
Social Media Management	Managing brand presence on social media	The brand engages with audience on social media platforms	AI can optimize post timing, personalize content for audience, and analyze engagement	Buffer, Hootsuite, Sprout Social
Digital Advertising	Advertising on digital platforms	Ads are created and displayed on various digital platforms	AI can automate ad placements, optimize ad spend, and provide ad performance insights	AdEspresso, Albert, Acquisio
User Experience (UX)	Ensuring positive interactions with digital platforms	Users interact with the brand's digital platforms	AI can personalize UX, provide insights into user behavior, and predict UX trends	Optimizely, Adobe Target, Apptentive

Data Analytics	Gaining insights from data	Data generated from digital interactions is analyzed	AI can provide real-time data insights, predict trends, and create reports	Tableau, Looker, Qlik
Cybersecurity	Protecting digital assets	Digital assets and data are protected from threats	AI can predict and identify threats, automate threat responses, and provide insights into potential vulnerabilities	Darktrace, CrowdStrike

Live Case Study
AI-Powered Digital Channel Launch and Scale Up

Figure 38 - Launching "QuirkyLook," an online clothing Store offering fun and unique AI-designed T-shirts (Source: Midjourney)

Context - Meet Sara, a young entrepreneur with a passion for fashion and a dream to launch her online clothing store, QuirkyLook. Sara's vision was to create a unique brand that catered to niche audiences, offering them t-shirts with designs that resonated with their interests. However, Sara had limited resources and knew that to make her dream a reality, she would need to leverage the power of AI. Here's how she did it:

✂ AI tools used:

- ChatGPT (For design research; content creation for website, products, social media, and email funnel)
- Midjourney (For t-shirt designs)
- Canva (For creating t-shirt mockup designs for social media ads)
- Avada (For email and WhatsApp marketing)
- Qikink (As print-on-demand vendor managing end-to-end fulfillment)
- Jasper AI (For copywriting)
- Notion AI (For task management and social media calendar)

💡 Step-by-Step Playbook

Step 1: Research Niches with ChatGPT:

Sara used **ChatGPT** to research potential niches for her online store. She identified anime, spiritual, animal-loving, and superhero themes as key niches popular among Indian consumers. ChatGPT helped her analyze market trends, customer preferences, and competitive landscape, providing valuable insights to shape her business strategy.

Step 2: T-Shirt Designs with Midjourney:

With her niches identified, Sara turned to **Midjourney**, an AI-powered design tool, to create unique t-shirt designs. Midjourney used generative AI to develop designs based on Sara's inputs, allowing her to quickly and efficiently create a diverse range of products for her store.

Figure 39 - T-Shirt Designs Generated with AI (Source: Midjourney)

Step 3: Sourcing with a Print-on-Demand Vendor:

Sara partnered with a print-on-demand vendor who managed the entire fulfillment process to allow her to focus on her core business without worrying about inventory management, shipping, and returns. The vendor's integration with AI tools enabled efficient order processing and timely delivery, enhancing customer satisfaction.

Sara could quickly generate mockups on the print-on-demand partner site with the designs created from **Midjourney** and then push those designs seamlessly to her **Shopify** store at the click of a button. Similarly, when the customer order came in, it would channel back to the POD partner site, and the entire fulfillment process would be auto-initiated. So, even as a Solopreneur, Sara could manage the whole operation 10x faster, powered by AI tools, as shown in the following steps.

Figure 40 - Print-on-Demand Vendor Site Mockup (Source: Qikink)

Step 4: Visualizing the Store with Figma:

Before creating her online store, Sara used **Figma**, a design tool for collaborative designing and prototyping. She created a flowchart to map out the user journey on her site, from landing on the homepage to making a purchase. She also used **Figma** to develop a website prototype, visualizing its appearance and function. This step ensured a user-friendly design and smooth navigation, enhancing the user experience.

Step 5: Create a Store on Shopify with Content from ChatGPT, Copy:

Sara used Shopify to set up her online store. She used ChatGPT and Jasper, AI-powered content writing tools, to create engaging product descriptions, compelling marketing copy, and informative blog posts. These tools helped her create high-quality content that resonated with her target audience, driving traffic to her store and boosting sales.

Figure 41 - Complete Store Content for QuirkyLook generated by AI
(Source: QuirkyLook.com)

Step 6: Email Marketing Drip with Avada:

Sara used Avada, an email marketing tool, to create an email marketing drip campaign. She used **ChatGPT** to design the welcome and abandoned cart email funnel. The AI-powered tool helped her craft personalized emails that engaged her customers, improved conversion rates, and increased customer loyalty.

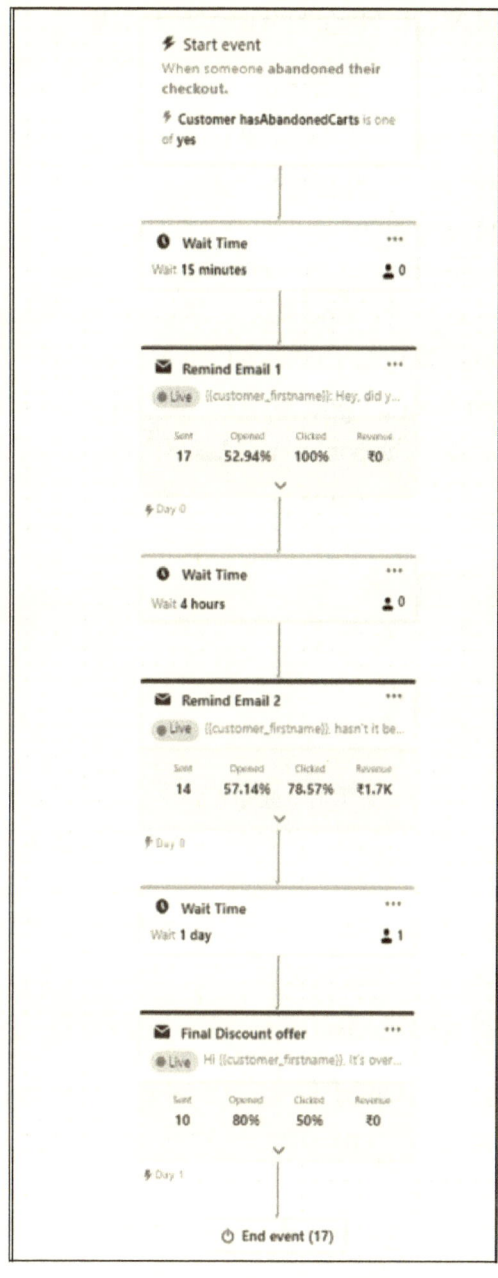

Figure 42 - Sample Abandoned Cart Email Sequence

Step 7: Social Media Handles with ChatGPT:

Sara used **ChatGPT** to manage her social media handles. The AI tool helped her create engaging posts, respond to customer queries, monitor social media trends, build a robust online presence, engage with her audience, and drive traffic to her store. Sara also used Notion AI to create the social media calendar and in-built automation to send task reminders and automated post-scheduling via Zapier. The social media calendar given below was generated with all post content within Notion at the click of a button (using the command 'Ask AI' and describing what to generate).

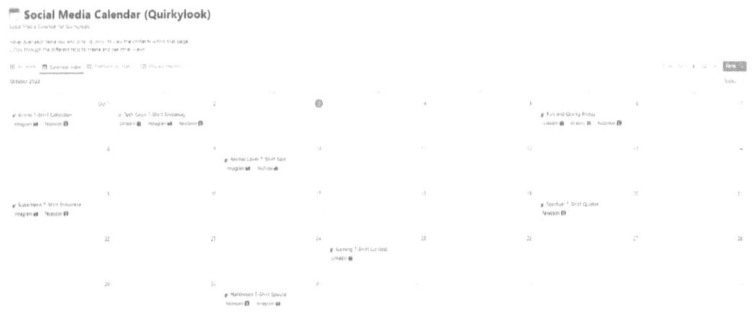

Figure 43 - Automated Social Media Calendar Generated on Notion AI

Step 8: Social Media Advertising with ChatGPT:

Sara also used **ChatGPT** to create effective Facebook and Instagram ad campaigns. The AI tool helped her identify the right target audience, craft compelling ad copy, set up pixels, and optimize her ad spend. This resulted in increased visibility, higher click-through rates, and improved conversion rates.

Step 9: Monitor, Streamline and Scale

Sara continued to monitor her business with in-built Shopify store analytics and her FB ad performance in the **Meta Ads Manager** dashboard. Adding the Facebook pixel helped her target the right customers as she scaled her ads by leveraging AI tools.

By leveraging AI, Sara could launch her online store 10 times faster and more efficiently than traditional methods. She could focus on her core business while AI cared for the rest. From market research and product design to content creation and digital marketing, AI played a crucial role in Sara's journey.

Sara's story is a testament to the power of AI in transforming businesses. It shows how AI can help businesses of all sizes, from solo entrepreneurs to large corporations, to go digital and thrive in the online marketplace. It demonstrates how AI can help businesses achieve more with less, enabling them to launch faster, scale quicker, and succeed in today's competitive digital landscape.

BEYOND THE OBVIOUS: AI IN FINANCE, LEGAL, PROJECT MANAGEMENT, AND MORE

> *"The future is already here — it's just not very evenly distributed."*
> *– William Gibson*

*A*s a leader in a large business venture, I had an opportunity to orchestrate a symphony of diverse teams from supply chain and marketing to legal, finance, research and development, project management, analytics, and more. Each of these teams played a crucial role in our enterprise's day-to-day operations and overall success, and managing this team was a mammoth task.

One of the most time-consuming tasks was managing contracts with our legal team. Every customer contract, product description, or public-facing document required meticulous drafting and multiple rounds of review. This often slowed our progress, impacting our time-to-market and hindering our efficiency.

In finance, the challenge was about more than just tracking revenue growth. It was about understanding the health of our bottom line, monitoring cash flows, and identifying opportunities for improvement. Monthly reviews with my CFO were insightful, but the sheer volume of data to be analyzed made the process slow and laborious.

As we ventured into new categories, the complexity of managing multiple projects surged. Every initiative required an intricate project management approach, from new product development to marketing campaigns and supply chain optimizations. I recall a particular initiative aimed at reducing manufacturing and product development costs, which involved managing multiple stakeholders, conducting follow-ups, and analyzing feedback, consuming a significant amount of our time.

In addition, public relations efforts required considerable time, whether it involved liaising with the press, preparing for interviews, participating in panel discussions, or crafting the right messages to convey. While crucial to our business, each task demanded a hefty share of our resources.

Looking back, I see how AI could have significantly enhanced our efficiency in these domains. With AI, contract management could be expedited, financial analysis could be more insightful, project management could be streamlined, and public relations could be optimized.

This chapter will explore how AI can be a game-changer in these other key business areas. With the right tools and a thoughtful approach, AI can help us automate or amplify our work in these areas, making them 10x more effective. As we delve deeper, we'll discover the potential of AI to revolutionize not just the prominent aspects of business but also the unsung heroes—legal, finance, project management, and more.

The Conventional Way

Traditionally, finance, legal, and project management functions have been manually intensive, often requiring specialized knowledge and skills. In finance, planning involves a delicate balance of analyzing past data, understanding cash flow dynamics, and forecasting future trends to ensure a healthy bottom line. Finance professionals must navigate a complex landscape of market fluctuations, economic conditions, and regulatory requirements. A single miscalculation in cash flow projections or budgeting can significantly impact profitability and liquidity.

Legal compliance, on the other hand, requires a deep and nuanced understanding of ever-changing laws and regulations. Legal documents are often reviewed and drafted by hand, a meticulous process where attention to detail is paramount, and the stakes are high. Any oversight can lead to compliance issues, legal disputes, or reputational damage. Also, functions like project management involve creating detailed project plans, tracking progress, and stakeholder management as some essential tasks.

However, these conventional methods have several drawbacks. The manual analysis of financial data, including cash flow management and budgeting, can be labor-intensive and time-consuming. This slows the process and makes it prone to errors, leading to financial losses or misalignment with strategic goals. The reliance on historical data and human intuition in economic forecasting, coupled with the subjective interpretation of legal texts, may only sometimes be accurate or reliable, lacking modern businesses' predictive insights to stay ahead.

Furthermore, manual processes can be challenging to scale, especially for growing businesses with increasing data and complexity. The intricate nature of financial analysis, the high stakes in legal compliance, and the multifaceted challenges of project management indicate a growing demand for technological innovation and automation in these critical business functions. The need for precise cash flow management, safeguarding the bottom line, and ensuring legal integrity underscores the limitations of traditional methods and the potential for transformative solutions in finance, legal, and project management.

Enter Artificial Intelligence

In the complex and demanding realms of finance, legal compliance, and project management, artificial intelligence (AI) emerges as a transformative force. With its ability to process vast amounts of data, make accurate predictions, and automate intricate tasks, AI redefines these critical business functions.

Finance: AI's impact on finance is profound. By employing advanced algorithms and machine learning, AI can analyze complex financial data, including cash flow patterns, market trends, and economic indicators, to provide real-time insights and forecasts. This leads to more accurate budgeting, risk assessment, and strategic planning, safeguarding the bottom line. AI-driven tools can also detect anomalies and potential fraud, enhancing financial security. Automating routine tasks, such as invoice processing and reconciliation, frees financial professionals to focus on value-added activities, driving efficiency and innovation.

Legal Compliance: In the legal domain, AI offers a new level of precision and efficiency. AI-powered legal tools can review contracts, regulations, and legal documents with unparalleled accuracy, identifying potential risks and compliance issues. Natural Language Processing (NLP) enables AI to understand and interpret complex legal language, providing insights that were previously attainable only through extensive human expertise. Document review and drafting automation reduces the time and effort involved, minimizing the risk of human error and enabling legal teams to respond more swiftly to emerging legal challenges.

Project Management: Project management, too, is ripe for AI-driven transformation. AI can analyze historical project data, progress, and external factors to predict potential delays, resource constraints, or other challenges. This predictive capability allows project managers to adjust strategies, proactively ensuring timely and successful project delivery. AI-powered collaboration tools facilitate seamless communication and coordination among team members, enhancing productivity and alignment with project goals.

AI is not just a technological advancement; it's a strategic enabler that unlocks new levels of efficiency, accuracy, and scalability in finance, legal, and project management. By leveraging AI, organizations can transcend the limitations of traditional methods, achieving a competitive edge in today's rapidly evolving business landscape. Integrating AI into these functions represents a paradigm shift, turning challenges into opportunities and paving the way for a future where data-driven decision-making, automation, and continuous improvement are the norms.

Real-Life Example:
KPMG: Investing in AI and Cloud Services for a Future-Ready Business

In a world where technology is rapidly reshaping industries, KPMG, one of the Big Four accounting firms, is boldly moving. The professional services company plans to invest $2 billion in artificial intelligence (AI) and cloud services across its business lines globally over the next five years. This investment is part of an expanded partnership with Microsoft, marking KPMG's commitment to harnessing the power of technology to revolutionize its operations.

This investment is not just about adopting new technologies but also transforming how KPMG operates. The company plans to automate its tax, audit, and consulting services, enabling employees to provide faster analysis and spend more time on strategic advice. The goal is to help more companies integrate AI into their operations, enhancing efficiency and productivity.

As part of the expanded partnership, KPMG will have early access to an AI assistant called Microsoft 365 Copilot before its launch to the general public. The company will also continue to use the Azure cloud platform, which it already uses OpenAI to build and run apps.

A significant portion of KPMG's investment will go toward generative AI, a technology many businesses are eager to apply to their finances to cut costs and yield new efficiencies. This technology will allow KPMG to strengthen its work related to environmental, social, and governance (ESG) issues by unifying massive data sets for tax reporting, analyzing potential ESG-related transactions, and performing data analysis for audits more timely.

KPMG's investment in AI and cloud services signals its commitment to staying ahead of the curve, leveraging technology to enhance its services, and preparing for a future where AI plays a central role in business operations.

AI-Enhanced Business Support Functions Transformation

Business Area	Area Description	What Happens	How AI Can Help	Example AI Tools
Finance	Managing the company's finances	Budgeting, forecasting, risk management, auditing, etc.	AI can automate data entry, provide predictive analytics for budgeting, detect financial fraud	QuickBooks, IBM Watson Financial Services
Legal	Managing the company's legal matters	Contract review, legal research, compliance checks, etc.	AI can automate contract analysis, assist in legal research, ensure regulatory compliance	Legal Robot, LawGeex

Project Management	Managing projects within the organization	Planning, executing, monitoring, and closing projects	AI can predict project risks, automate task assignments, provide real-time project analytics	Asana, Trello
Public Relations	Managing the brand's public image	Press release distribution, media contact management, crisis management, etc.	AI can optimize press release timing, track media mentions, and predict PR crises.	Meltwater, PRMax

Live Case Study
Revolutionizing Project Management with AI

Figure 44 - Autom8AI image generated by AI (Source: Midjourney)

Context: Meet Sam, the project manager at Autom8AI, a thriving SaaS solutions company. Sam is responsible for overseeing various projects, coordinating with different teams, ensuring timely delivery, and maintaining the quality of work. However, as the company grew, manually managing these tasks became increasingly challenging. Recognizing the potential of AI, Sam decided to transform project management operations at Autom8AI. Here's how he did it:

🛠 AI tools used:

- ChatGPT (For legal documents, customer support and project planning)
- Trello (For project management)
- Slack (For customer support)
- Zapier (For automation)
- Google Sheet (For storing entries based on the Google form inputs)
- Botpress (For automated customer support and issue resolution)

💡 Step-by-Step Playbook

Step 1: Project Planning

Sam started by automating the project planning process. Once a customer or team member submitted a Google form with all the required details, the information was channeled to Google Sheets as a new row entry. Using **Google Sheets**, **ChatGPT**, and **Zapier**, Sam created a system where project details, timelines, and team assignments were automatically populated into a project plan created by ChatGPT. This saved time and ensured that all project details were accurately recorded.

Step 2: Documentation

Sam used ChatGPT to create legal and other necessary documentation for every new customer. For instance, when a customer signed up, an automated sequence started with Zapier to create documents like Contract Terms and Conditions, NDA,

Business proposal, etc., as needed for a specific case. Sam also used AI tools like Humata to quickly understand the brief or highlight of any process documents or SOP (Standard Operating Procedure) shared by the customer.

Step 3: Task Assignment

Next, Sam used Trello, a project management tool integrated with **Zapier**, to automate task assignments. When a new project task was added to the Google Sheet and ChatGPT created a project plan, Zapier created a new card in the Trello board for the project, and tasks were automatically assigned to team members, along with due dates, descriptions, relevant links, states, etc. based on the project plan.

*Notion is an alternate AI tool that can be used for project management, especially given its integrated AI capabilities. The utilization of Trello in this case study showcases the capability of AI-powered tools at the disposal of businesses. It is imperative for business owners and leaders to grasp the 'HOW,' and fortunately, there's a vast array of tools catering to the 'WHO,' ready to propel operations to new heights.

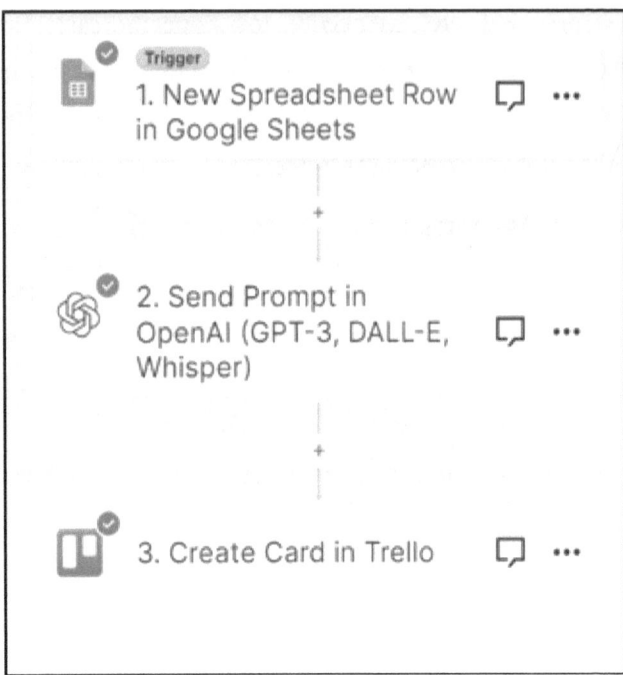

Figure 45 - Zapier Automation

Step 4: Progress Tracking

Sam used **Trello**'s built-in automation tool to track each task's progress. It allowed Sam to set up rules, buttons, and commands to automate various actions on Trello, such as follow-ups, status tracker, and moving a task to "Done" when a team member marked it as complete.

Step 5: Customer Support

For effective communication, Sam integrated **Slack** with ChatGPT using Zapier. He trained CHATGPT on the company documents, and whenever the customer asked a question on the Slack channel, it automatically routed for ChatGPT to respond in the support assistant avatar defined by Sam, which helped automate the complete customer support and only escalated cases that could not be answered by the AI tool.

Step 6: Issue Resolution

For internal purposes as well, Sam used **Botpress** to automate the first level of issue resolution. Whenever a team member reported an issue on Slack, Botpress chatbot was used to provide initial troubleshooting steps. This helped resolve minor issues quickly and freed up time for the team to focus on more complex problems.

By integrating AI into project management, Sam was able to streamline operations, improve communication, and enhance productivity at Autom8AI. This case study serves as a blueprint for other project managers looking to leverage AI in their operations. The use of simple yet powerful tools like Google Sheets, Zapier, Trello, Slack, Botpress, and ChatGPT demonstrates the transformative potential of AI in project management.

TAKING THE LEAP - EMBRACING AI IN YOUR BUSINESS JOURNEY

"You don't have to see the whole staircase, just take the first step."
– Martin Luther King Jr

*A*s we conclude this exploration of AI's transformative potential, it's clear that we're not discussing a fleeting trend or a buzzword that will fade into obscurity. AI is a powerful reality, a force already reshaping our world and how we conduct business. We've traversed a vast landscape, delving into practical strategies and real-world examples illustrating AI's profound impact.

Our journey began with a fundamental understanding of AI, its essence, and its boundless potential. We've seen how AI can act as a catalyst, unlocking your leadership potential and revolutionizing every facet of your business, from market research to product development, sales, business development, customer experience enhancement, and beyond.

We've witnessed AI's capacity to drive 10x efficiency, facilitate data-driven decisions, and deliver unparalleled personalization to meet and exceed customer expectations. We've also explored AI's transformative influence in diverse fields such as learning and development, business process automation, and more.

Having navigated the vast expanse of AI and its myriad applications, it's time for you, as business owners, founders, and leaders, to take the leap and embrace AI in your business journey.

AI is not a magic wand that instantly solves all business challenges. It's a powerful tool that requires investment - in time, effort, and resources. But the potential rewards—reduced operational costs, improved efficiency, increased customer satisfaction, and the ability to drive innovation—are well worth the investment.

Embracing AI doesn't necessitate a degree in computer science or a deep understanding of machine learning algorithms. Start small with the user-friendly AI tools we've discussed. Experience firsthand how they can transform various aspects of your business. The key is to start; there's no better time than now.

Let this book serve as your guide, your roadmap into the world of AI. As we stand on the precipice of this new era, remember that every journey begins with a single step. It's time to take that step, embrace AI, and harness its power for your business journey.

As you embark on or continue your journey with AI, it's essential to remember that AI alone cannot solve all business challenges. Instead, it should be viewed as a tool to augment human capabilities, increasing efficiency and allowing individuals to focus on tasks that demand creativity, empathy, and strategic thinking.

AI Application Checklist 2.0

We can also use this more advanced checklist to review various aspects of our business to guide our decisions on AI implementation. Each element is scored from 1 to 10, with a higher score suggesting a solid case for AI implementation.

Aspect	Question	Scoring Score 1-10 (10 if favorable, 1 if not)
Task Nature	Is the task repetitive and rule-based? Does it require high precision and consistency?	
Data Availability	Is there enough quality data available for training the AI? Is this data correctly labeled and free from biases?	
Data Privacy	How will the application of AI affect data privacy? Are there any legal or ethical implications to consider?	

Cost Evaluation	What is the estimated cost of implementing AI? This includes the cost of data preparation, model training, model deployment, and maintenance.	
Benefits Estimation	How much time will be saved by automating this task? How much additional revenue could be generated? Could the AI solution lead to new business opportunities or improved customer satisfaction?	
Risk Analysis	What risks are associated with AI implementation, such as increased cybersecurity threats, customer backlash, or regulatory issues?	

Feasibility Check	Is the necessary infrastructure available to support AI? Are there enough skilled staff members to manage and maintain the AI system? Is the organization's culture ready for the change?	
Implementation Timeline	How long will it take to implement the AI solution? This should consider data preparation, model development, integration, and testing time.	
Return on Investment	Will the benefits from the AI system exceed the total cost of implementation in a reasonable timeframe?	
Impact on Employees	How will the AI implementation impact the workforce? Will there be job displacement, or will it create new opportunities for upskilling?	

Add up your scores to get an overall rating out of 100. A higher score suggests a strong case for AI implementation, while a lower score suggests that further analysis may be needed before proceeding. Please note that the scoring system should be adapted based on your company's priorities. For example, if data privacy is vital for your company, you should weigh that aspect more heavily.

Armed with this toolkit, you are now ready to explore the boundless possibilities of AI to 10x your business impact and growth.

My final advice to you is to start small but think big. Begin with smaller projects to gain confidence and understand the nuances of AI. But keep sight of the big picture—aim for comprehensive digital transformation.

In closing, remember this: AI is not an enemy to be feared but a companion for the journey ahead, a tool to be wielded wisely, and a friend to help you unlock your potential and that of your business.

In the AI-enabled future, businesses that will truly stand out will be those that not only adopt AI but adapt to it, making it an intrinsic part of their strategic decision-making. This is your time to be part of that group of pioneers.

The future of AI is here, and it is teeming with potential. As a business leader, the only question remains: Are you ready to leap?

The AI revolution awaits your participation. Embrace, harness, and let it propel your business into a future of unprecedented growth and success.

MASTERMIND COURSE - EMPOWERING YOUR ENTREPRENEURIAL JOURNEY WITH AI

The story of entrepreneurship is one of grit, determination, and the audacious belief that you can shape your destiny. As an entrepreneur, you are the hero of this story, armed with an idea, ready to conquer the business world.

Yet, even heroes need a secret weapon, a force multiplier that gives them an edge. In the narrative of modern business, this game-changing tool is artificial intelligence (AI). It's no longer a futuristic concept but a present reality, reshaping industries and redefining how we do business.

However, understanding AI and effectively harnessing it for your business are two different stories. That's where our journey together continues, transitioning from AI enlightenment to AI empowerment.

Introducing the Mastermind Course: Ignite Your AI Superpowers

Welcome to the Mastermind Course, a transformative, 30-day intensive journey meticulously designed for aspiring entrepreneurs like you who are set to disrupt the world with their ideas. This is not just an educational course but a hands-on workshop, a collaborative community, and a personal mentorship experience all rolled into one.

For a month, we'll navigate the maze of AI applications in business, moving beyond the theoretical to the practical. Together, we'll solve real-world business problems, work on concrete projects, and design AI strategies tailored to your unique entrepreneurial vision.

Throughout this journey, you won't be alone. You'll be part of a community of like-minded people eager to share ideas, insights, and experiences. And most importantly, I'll be there with you every step of the way.

Imagine the wealth you could create by being 10x more efficient. Imagine the freedom you could enjoy by automating repetitive tasks. The Mastermind Course is your ticket to this extraordinary future.

So, are you ready to leap? Are you prepared to step into the future, embrace AI, and lead your business into a new era of growth and prosperity?

If your answer is yes, join the Mastermind Course and embark on this exciting journey.

This is your moment, your opportunity to take control of your future. Are you ready to make it count? Let's leap together.

Sign up for the Mastermind Course here → https://aipreneurcoach.com/masterclass

Figure 46 - Scan the Code to Sign up for AI Masterclass

BONUS - 10 READY TO USE AI-DRIVEN BUSINESS LAUNCH TEMPLATES

Embarking on the entrepreneurial journey is akin to setting sail on the high seas. It's thrilling, challenging, and filled with the promise of treasure. But to navigate these waters successfully, you need a compass. Here are the critical mantras for success as an entrepreneur:

1. **Passion is your North Star:** Love what you do, and you'll never work a day. Passion fuels perseverance, and perseverance paves the way to success.
2. **Embrace the journey:** Success is not a destination; it's a journey. Celebrate the small victories, learn from the setbacks, and keep moving forward.
3. **Innovation is your sail:** In the sea of business, innovation catches the wind. It propels you forward, sets you apart, and guides you to uncharted territories.

4. **Resilience is your anchor:** The seas will not always be calm. Resilience will keep you grounded during the storms and help you sail through.
5. **Learning is your map:** The world is changing quickly. Continuous learning will help you adapt, evolve, and stay ahead of the curve.

You may feel it's too late and you don't have the skill or resources. You might have no idea or team to start a business. Let's equip you with the resources required to build your own business. Powered by AI, the entrepreneurial landscape is dotted with inspiring success stories of solopreneurs who have built million-dollar companies from scratch.

To help you start thinking about which business may be right for you, **let me quote this Japanese concept of Ikigai**, which is the intersection of what you love, what you're good at, what the world needs, and what you can be paid for. It's about finding fulfillment, happiness, and balance in your actions. When starting a business, the Ikigai mantra can be your guiding light.

1. **What You Love (Your Passion):** Start a business around something you're passionate about. It could be anything from writing to fitness, from cooking to coding.
2. **What You're Good At (Your Skill):** Leverage your skills and expertise to offer a product or service that stands out in the market.
3. **What The World Needs (The Market Demand):** Identify a problem that needs solving, a gap that needs filling, or a trend on the rise. Your business should address a real need or desire in the market.

4. **What You Can Be Paid For (The Business Model):** Develop a business model to monetize your passion and skills effectively. This could involve selling products, offering services, running ads, affiliate marketing, or any other revenue-generating strategy that fits your business.

Remember, the sweet spot for starting a business that can flourish lies at the intersection of these four elements. Find your Ikigai, and you'll find your path to entrepreneurial success.

BUSINESS IDEAS FOR NEWBIES

Discover the transformative power of AI in the realm of business. Whether you're a student, a homemaker, or a professional seeking a fresh start, here are ten business ideas tailored for minimal resources but with maximum impact.

Business Idea 1: E-Book Creation

Harness AI tools like ChatGPT to craft an engaging e-book on a topic close to your heart. Dive deep into subjects, create compelling narratives, and then utilize platforms like Amazon and Etsy to reach a broad audience eager for fresh content.

Business Idea 2: Freelancing

Offer your unique skills on platforms like Fiverr and Upwork. Whether you're a graphic designer, writer, or digital marketer, there's a global audience seeking your expertise. AI can help streamline your services and enhance deliverables.

Business Idea 3: Online Coaching

Empower others with your knowledge through personalized coaching sessions. Use messaging platforms for communication and let AI tools assist in scheduling, feedback analysis, and content creation, ensuring each session is impactful.

Business Idea 4: Story Writing

Channel your inner storyteller with the assistance of AI tools like ChatGPT. Craft captivating tales, explore diverse genres, and market them on platforms like Amazon Kindle or your website.

Business Idea 5: Blogging

Carve a niche in the blogging world on a topic you're passionate about. AI can assist in content creation, SEO optimization, and even design, ensuring your blog stands out in the digital crowd.

Business Idea 6: Affiliate Marketing

Venture into the lucrative world of affiliate marketing. With AI's analytical prowess, optimize your website for conversions, track user behavior, and refine your strategies for maximum revenue.

Business Idea 7: E-commerce

Dive into the e-commerce wave with an AI-backed store. From identifying trending products to setting optimal pricing and managing inventory, AI ensures your store runs smoothly and profitably.

Business Idea 8: Social Media

Establish a magnetic social media presence. Use AI to craft engaging posts, schedule content, and analyze engagement metrics, ensuring your brand resonates with its audience.

Business Idea 9: Translation Services

Bridge global communication gaps by offering AI-powered translation services. Cater to businesses and individuals alike, ensuring accurate and culturally sensitive translations.

Business Idea 10: Career Coaching

Guide job seekers to their dream roles. With AI's assistance, craft standout resumes, offer mock interviews, and provide actionable feedback, ensuring your clients are well-prepared for their career pursuits.

Now that we've explored these inspiring and easy-to-launch business ideas, it's time to equip you with the tools to launch your chosen venture successfully. Check out AI-driven business launch templates, a complete step-by-step toolkit common to any business you decide to build. These templates will serve as your compass, guiding you through each phase of your entrepreneurial journey.

BONUS TEMPLATES

Refer to all bonus templates here → https://businessaitoolkit.com/powerhouse

Template 1: Market and Niche Research

Every successful journey begins with a clear destination. Use AI to conduct comprehensive market research and identify a niche that aligns with your passion and expertise. AI-powered analytics will uncover valuable insights about your target audience, competitors, and emerging trends, laying the groundwork for a business that resonates with your customers.

Template 2: The Business Blueprint

A solid plan is your guiding star in business. Leverage AI to create a comprehensive business blueprint that outlines your mission, vision, objectives, and strategies. AI-powered tools will assist you in generating data-driven forecasts, risk assessments, and financial projections, providing you with a roadmap to navigate the challenges and seize the opportunities ahead.

Template 3: Supplier or Vendor Development

Launching a business often involves establishing partnerships with suppliers and vendors. Let AI assist you in identifying reliable suppliers, comparing prices, and evaluating the quality of products or services. AI-driven supplier discovery will ensure you align with partners who can fuel your venture's growth.

Template 4: Your Digital Platform

In the digital age, your business platform is the bridge that connects you to your audience. Use AI to build a user-friendly website or e-commerce platform and optimize it for search engines with AI-driven SEO tools. Additionally, AI can support you in crafting compelling content that engages and converts visitors into loyal customers.

Template 5: High Conversion Sales Page

Your sales page is your guiding light for potential customers. Employ AI to create a high-conversion sales page that captivates visitors and drives them to take action. AI-powered copywriting tools will help you craft persuasive, personalized content that resonates with your audience.

Template 6: Legal Toolkit

Navigating the legal landscape is crucial for your business's protection and compliance. Use AI to generate essential legal documents such as privacy policies, terms of service, and contracts. AI-driven legal assistance will ensure you launch your business on solid legal ground.

Template 7: Sales Funnel Optimization

An efficient sales funnel is the pathway that guides prospects toward becoming loyal customers. With AI, you can optimize your sales funnel, from lead generation to conversion and retention. AI-driven tools will analyze customer behavior and preferences, enabling you to tailor your funnel for maximum impact.

Template 8: Marketing Resources

In the interconnected realm of social media and messaging apps, AI is your most potent ally in reaching and engaging your target audience. Utilize AI to develop personalized marketing campaigns across social media platforms and messaging apps. AI-powered analytics will help you measure campaign performance and refine your strategies for stellar results.

Template 9: Talent Acquisition

As your business grows, the right talent will be your fuel. Employ AI to create a talent roadmap, identifying your team's critical roles and skill requirements. AI-driven candidate screening and assessment will ensure that you assemble a stellar crew that propels your business to new heights.

Template 10: Scaling Your Business

As your business gains momentum, scalability becomes the key to your success. AI will be instrumental in automating repetitive tasks, optimizing operations, and enhancing productivity. Moreover, AI can assist in preparing data-driven reports and presentations to attract investors who believe in your vision and are eager to be a part of your journey.

With these ten AI-driven business launch templates, you have a complete toolkit to turn your entrepreneurial dreams into reality. Each template is a force of innovation designed to simplify complex processes and amplify your capabilities. So, embrace the AI era, let these business ideas and templates be your guiding stars, and embark on a journey to build a prosperous and transformative future.

The possibilities are limitless, and with AI as your co-pilot, the path to success is brighter than ever!

Figure 47 - Scan Code to Access the Bonus Toolkit

www.ingramcontent.com/pod-product-compliance
Lightning Source LLC
LaVergne TN
LVHW091630070526
838199LV00044B/1011